Reaping God's Harvest

Equipping the Church for Evangelism

Yan Hadley

New Wine Press

New Wine Press
PO Box 17
Chichester
England PO20 6YB

ISBN: 1 874367 16 7

Typeset by CRB (Drayton) Typesetting Services, Norwich
Printed in England by Clays Ltd, St Ives plc

Dedication

This book is dedicated to the three most important and loved people in my life, next to that of Jesus Christ. My wife Lorrainne and my daughters Claire and Naomi who have enriched my life in every possible way.

Contents

Acknowledgements

My grateful thanks go to all that God has used to motivate me in writing this book. The support and encouragement, especially of my wife Lorrainne, without which this would not have been completed, has been deeply appreciated.

Also the invaluable help of Lesley Hullet, Gill Lewis, Janet Curtis, Anneka Western and Martine Finney, who laboured willingly in typing, to relieve the work load on my wife.

My gratitude goes also to my good friend David Adams, who gave of his time to proof read most of the manuscript.

Last and certainly not least, I give thanks to God for my precious daughters, Claire and Naomi. They tried hard to be patient about the absence of their dad, when attention, play and simply time together was wanted.

Foreword

I have known Yan Hadley for many years, and have worked with him closely when he was part of my team; *Reaping God's Harvest* is exactly what I would have expected from Yan. This is not a book of theory, but one in which Yan writes from his own experience, about the methods of evangelism that God has called him to do.

Yan's motivation is to get every believer doing that work which is so close to God's heart – the winning of the lost. I agree with him when he writes that so much is being talked about in evangelism but not enough is being done. Yan has written this book to get people active in evangelism rather than just thinking about it. The teaching is basic and practical so that anyone can easily pick up the book and use it to help them reach the people they live amongst.

One of the things which impressed me most in reading through the book, was that Yan's personal integrity comes through. There is no pretence here, what you read is the experience of a man who has been actively involved in a wide range of evangelism for many years. Yan has proved for himself that these methods are effective. He has worked hard in the 'harvest fields' as one of those labourers God has called. *Reaping God's Harvest* is a powerful testimony to the fruits of diligent, patient evangelism.

There is still an important place for streetwork, open air meetings and house to house visitation in the evangelistic strategy of every church. Yan also writes about newer ideas like friendship evangelism. It was good to note the safeguards Yan gives in this, which I would recommend every believer should pay close attention to. There is also a very useful chapter on the good news of God's healing power which can be a very effective method of reaching unchurched people.

Some of the things in this book you may have heard or read before, but I am convinced that Yan will motivate you to get more involved in evangelism. I commend the book to you.

Don Double
Director of Good News Crusade

1

'Every Believer a Witness'

A few years ago while browsing around a Christian book-shop I came across something that both amused and challenged me. It was a bright poster of a very large yawning hippopotamus. The caption underneath, in bold black letters was, 'when all is said and done, ... there's a lot more said than done!' That really seemed to sum up much of the evangelistic fervour in Christianity then, and today is still a very true reflection of the state of the Church in some areas.

One of the most disturbing things evident in the lives of Christians, even where God's Spirit is said to be moving, is this lack of action in evangelism. I believe we need to question very seriously those who claim to be renewed in the Holy Spirit if their experience isn't bringing a renewal of vision for the lost. In the same way, we should challenge the genuineness of a church that says it is moving in restoration if part of that emphasis isn't restoring back to them a willing zeal to share Christ with others. Those who claim to be baptised in the Holy Spirit and speak in tongues but don't have the powerful evidence of being a witness for Jesus have missed what Acts 1:8 is all about. The *'receiving'* of the Holy Spirit which every Christian likes to hear about is only half the story. We have received God's gifts of grace for a purpose, that we might be, *'His witnesses'*. Evangelism was never intended to be the peculiar hobby of a few individuals but rather the perpetual task of the whole Church!

Someone has calculated that if Billy Graham were to have a crusade meeting every night, where a thousand people were won to Christ each evening, it would take him one hundred and twenty seven years to see Britain converted. But if every born again believer won just one person to Christ every year, the entire nation would be Christians in less than eight years!

The marked contrast between evangelism today and what we find in the early Church is this: we talk about it, they did it! Today people listen to messages and read books on evangelism, go to conferences and camps where they feel moved by God to do something, but at the end of it all, very little is actually done. In a day and age where everything is so complex and our minds continually bombarded with systems, strategies and techniques, we need to get back to the simple New Testament principle of witnessing. That is, every individual believer making a whole-hearted response to what the Lord Jesus has commissioned them to do, in a natural way, through everyday living. Sharing our faith should never be something that is unnatural. Rather it should be very much part of our lifestyle – in fact it ought to be as natural to witness as it is to breathe. We don't need to think much about our breathing, we just do it without any difficulty. So too witnessing should have this naturalness about it.

The apostle Paul was able to say,

> *'I am not ashamed of the gospel: it is the power of God for salvation to everyone who has faith.'*
>
> (Romans 1:16)

That is a very bold statement to make, but we see the reality of those words in the fearless way that he went about speaking of Christ. When Paul stood before King Agrippa he had absolute confidence to say,

'I was not disobedient to the heavenly vision, but declared first to those at Damascus, then at Jerusalem and throughout all the country of Judea, and also to the gentiles, that they should repent and turn to God and perform deeds worthy of their repentance.'

(Acts 26:19–20)

Paul wasn't disobedient to what the Lord had told him to do. I believe that God requires each one of us to respond in the same way with what He made so clear is His will. This should be a priority goal in our life, one that we work towards with all the energy He mightily inspires within us.

Each of us needs to use every God-given opportunity to witness for Christ. Notice that I say, 'God given opportunity'. I don't believe that the Lord would have us go recklessly sharing Christ in an insensitive way for He clearly tells us in His word that, *'there is a time to keep silence, and a time to speak'* (Ecclesiastes 3:7). I do feel though that the understanding we need to have today is that *'there is a time to speak!'*

In the book of Acts we find that Peter and John have been arrested and brought before the religious leaders to give an account of why they have been preaching Christ. These people did not need counselling on how to share their faith. Their enthusiastic witness came out of the relationship they had with Jesus.

Because the Lord was so real and precious to them it was just very natural to share what they had discovered. They were talking about the most important person in their life. Someone who had died for them but was now miraculously alive again, a close friend that had brought a tremendous change into their lives. So when the religious leaders told Peter and John not to share their faith, never to speak out in the name of Jesus again, Peter didn't hesitate to reply. He said in amazement, *'we cannot but speak of what we have seen and heard'* (Acts 4:20).

This burning conviction can only flow out of a close

13

intimate relationship with the Lord. We see this same attitude stirring the heart of John:

> *'That which was from the beginning, which we have heard, which we have seen with our eyes, which we have looked at and our hands have touched – this we proclaim concerning the Word of Life.'*
>
> (1 John 1:1, NIV)

Those things that John had experienced personally he was able to share with no difficulty at all.

We should never testify to Christ out of a sense of obligation, but rather because He has so captured our heart we speak of Him readily, earnestly and enthusiastically. If any of us find difficulty in sharing our faith, then we have to go back to the root of the matter, our relationship with the Lord. He alone is able to change us so that we have that irrepressible zeal! As the great preacher C.H. Spurgeon used to say, 'Get on fire for God and people will soon come and watch you burn!' This might seem to over-simplify a complicated issue so let us take a look at some of the problems which are a hindrance to evangelism.

'Come In and Be Saved'

Very common in the Church but quite absent in the New Testament is the 'come in and be saved approach' to evangelism. This can be a major blockage to our effectiveness in seeing others won to Christ. We need to think more in terms of going out to where people are and reaching the unreached for Christ. Jesus taught in a parable that we were to, *'go out to the highways and hedges and compel people to come in'* (Luke 14:23). The command of Jesus was always to, *'go into all the world and preach the gospel'* (Mark 16:15). Crusades and Church gospel meetings should never be a substitute for our witnessing. They may be a legitimate conclusion to all our hard work, but never an alternative for personal evangelism. We read, '*A sower went out to sow*' (Matthew 13:3). There must be that '*going out*' with the seed of God's precious word and planting it into the soil of people's lives, for the soil will not come to the seed!

It is not enough just to deliver invitations through people's letter boxes, place an advert in the newspaper or put up posters in the local shops. If this is all we do then we achieve little but spend our money and appease our conscience. It is necessary to show the unsaved that we really care and are concerned about them, not just as 'lost souls' but as individuals. Where could we do this better than over the garden fence chatting to our neighbours, or in our own front room with a cup of coffee, in the office with colleagues at work, and with the people we meet down at the local shops. We are only really effective when the initial contact has been made on neutral territory and on their level of understanding, rather than expecting them to jump straight in to where we are. It is in this environment rather than in a Church building that we need to begin sowing God's word in love, with sensitivity and consistency.

There are countless thousands of people who will never darken the door of a Church, except perhaps on special occasions, because the building is cold, and uninviting. Even when leaders go to the expense of brightening up the place and making the building more comfortable, still that has little effect because of the various cultural differences between the Church and unchurched people. No matter how hard we try, often the terms and words we use are a foreign language to the uninitiated. The forms of worship in our meeting may be very precious to the Christian but quite alien to the outsider. Many of our Church practices only leave the unsaved confused, not knowing quite what they should or shouldn't do.

These differences can cause them to feel very insecure and to say the least, a little strange and out of place. It is therefore not surprising that people much prefer the independence of their own homes and the security of their own territory. I don't believe we can expect to see significant results from the 'come in' way of thinking, until we have first gone out to where people are. When we have sat where they sit, enabling them to see that we are human and not quite as unusual as at first they thought, then the breakthrough we long for becomes more likely.

'I'm Not Qualified'

Another barrier that prevents many Christians today from witnessing is the misunderstanding that it is the Pastor's job, the missionary's responsibility, the full-time worker's or the 'evangelist's' calling – and theirs alone. The thinking that 'they're qualified and I'm not so I can't evangelize' is quite wrong. What God is reminding Christians of today I believe, is that ordinary church members are to be the principal ambassadors of the gospel. It is not just for the 'professionals': their task is to equip church members to witness and be effective in the work of the ministry, not to do all the work themselves.

The way we see ourselves is a very significant part of the problem. Too often people's view of themselves is less than God's. We need to look at ourselves as He sees us. For example, Abraham saw himself as a childless old man, but God saw him as the father of many nations. Gideon saw himself as the least in his family and his clan as the weakest. God saw him as a mighty man of valour. Moses saw himself as an inadequate and inarticulate leader but God saw him as the deliverer of His people Israel. Believing God's word rather than our fears or other people's opinions releases us to grow into our full potential. As the simple words of a well known American song puts it,

'You are a promise, you are a possibility,
You are a promise, with a capital "P",
You are a great big bundle of potentiality!'

The qualifications for effective witnessing are not a first class education, three years training at a Bible college or a degree in theology. These things can be a tremendous asset but if they are all we have then they will always get in the way of our communicating the life of Christ.

What we need is a personal relationship with Jesus as Lord and the Baptism in the Holy Spirit, enduing us with power from on high. This enables the gospel to come to people,

> *'not only in word, but also in power and in the Holy Spirit and with full conviction.'*
>
> (1 Thessalonians 1:5)

Peter and John were *'uneducated and common men'* (Acts 4:13), quite unqualified in themselves to testify to the resurrection of Jesus Christ. They were nothing special, just simple fishermen, but it was their personal knowledge of Christ and the anointing of the Holy Spirit that made them so effective. They were able to reveal Jesus to the rulers, elders and scribes, Annas the high priest, Caiaphas, John and Alexander and all who were of the high priestly family. By God's power they were part of the team that began to turn the world upside down!

Paul's words to Timothy were, *'Do the work of an evangelist'* (2 Timothy 4:5). Now Timothy certainly wasn't an 'evangelist', but Paul encouraged him to do this work. We likewise must not be over concerned with qualifications, nor even be anxious about not having all the answers, but simply start with what Jesus has done for us. An evangelist is simply someone who passes on the good news of the gospel to others. We would find very little difficulty if we received an inheritance of a million pounds to share the joy of our discovery. There would be no fear of rejection, no anxiety of ridicule, no doubts as to our ability to articulate how we felt. We would have an excitement, a confidence and a conviction as we spoke of the good news. When we are gripped by all that our inheritance in Christ means, how much more should we be excited to share with those that we meet?

'We Are Not Ready Yet for Evangelism'

Another major problem that hinders evangelism is that of being too introspective. An over-emphasis on getting the Church 'right' before any outward proclamation is considered, in many cases paralyses the Church, and is a subtle deception of the enemy. We shouldn't be asking the question, 'which is more important, to develop Christian character in the Church or be declaring Christ's gospel to the world?' It is as foolish to ask, 'which of the two wings of an aeroplane are the most necessary, the right or the left?' Both, of course, are vital if we are to get anywhere. So too, character and proclamation go hand in hand if we are to make any progress in our Christian life. Sheep need not only feeding and protection to grow strong, but also exercise. Without exercise they would only grow weak, lazy and sick. This is something that can be seen in evidence throughout our country today in the lives of Christians and churches which neglect evangelism.

It is of course a righteous goal to want to be seen as godly before being heard. However if we wait until we are 'ready' and 'have got it all together' in our walk with God and our relating to one another, then little will be accomplished for His Kingdom. We must start where we are, *'prepared always to give an account for the hope that is within us'*, being *'instant in season and out of season'*, witnessing with a commitment to live out daily what we preach.

As we get on and do what we have been commissioned to in sharing Christ then our character is strengthened and the Church grows together in maturity. If you want to see your congregation develop and relationships deepen, then get them active in looking out to others. Unity and maturity are forged in action! The Christians at Thessalonica are an excellent example of this point. They hadn't been converted long but the testimony of their lifestyle and proclamation was very evident. Paul says to them,

> 'you became an example to all the believers in Macedo'nia and Acha'ia. For not only has the word of the Lord sounded forth from you in Macedo'nia and Acha'ia, but your faith in God has gone forth everywhere, so that we need not say anything.'
>
> (1 Thessalonians 1:7–8)

This growth came not through sitting hand in hand examining their weaknesses but through speaking out boldly for Christ and standing firmly together against persecution.

'It Isn't My Particular Gift'

Our next hurdle is the classic cop-out which people often offer as an excuse for their lack of evangelism. 'It isn't my gift, my ministry is counselling' or 'I'm a deacon, Sunday school teacher, youth worker, administrator, musician, etc.' This attitude is similar to the second problem we mentioned, of those who say 'I'm not qualified', but there is a difference. Often the people who shy away from involvement in evangelism with the excuse of their lack of qualifications are doing very little else in the church; there tends to be no activity from them in any area of responsibility. But the people we are thinking of now are normally busy in the Church and have particular responsibilities which they feel called to. Their conclusion is that anything outside of that calling can't be their 'gifting', so they are excused.

There is one major reason for witnessing – Jesus told us all to do it! What God is calling us to has got nothing to do with our gifting, or our natural talents. The Bible tells us that we are to be 'witnesses'. So what we are talking about is the willingness to bear testimony for Jesus Christ. This is something that God expects each one of us to do and He will always equip us for it with His ability.

A witness is simply somebody who states those things that he has seen, heard and experienced at first hand, those things which he knows to be true. Take the example of an accident, when witnesses are called to court. These people do not testify to what they think might have occurred nor to what they think should have taken place. They are required only to speak of what they know actually happened, what they have seen with their eyes and heard with their ears. This is all God wants of us and indeed it's something that we are all able to do. The scriptural pattern is to start where you are geographically and then work outwards – *'Jerusalem and in all Judea and Samaria and to the end of the earth'* (Acts 1:8). Begin in your street, place of work, college or school and let God make you a witness through your particular gifts and talents there.

'But I'm a Shy Person'

The last stumbling block we need to consider is our human nature, which is sometimes controlled by fear. Frequently I've heard people say 'I'm not an extrovert, I'm reserved'. People at times hide behind their personality when it suits them as an excuse for not doing what they know they should. But there are also those who really can't witness effectively because they are in bondage to their personality. As far as our old nature is concerned we are reluctant to do or say anything which might seem by the majority to be out of place. This should be brought to God in prayer for it will always be a hindrance in our witnessing. We are a *'new creation'* (2 Corinthians 5:17). Just as the apostle Paul told Timothy, *'God did not give us a spirit of timidity but a spirit of power!'* (2 Timothy 1:7). If we rely on what we were like or what we are expected to be, the so called 'norm' or 'acceptable' way of living, then we will be less effective as we try to witness.

God in Christ has recreated us to fulfil His purpose and plan for our life. We have a new nature to develop into all that He's called us to be. Our prayer should be the same as that of the early Christians, *'Grant to thy servants to speak thy word with all boldness'* (Acts 4:29). The boldness which was evident in the early Church, is a godly characteristic that ought to be in our lives today.

The wisdom of Solomon tells us that, *'The righteous are bold as a lion'* (Proverbs 28:1). During the course of my ministry I've been to East Africa and have come quite close to uncaged lions. It is a fact you will never see a lion tip-toeing through the jungle, nervously twitching at every rustle in the bushes and breaking into a cold sweat at all the different sounds around. We know that the lion strides through the jungle with its head held high, and at frequent intervals there comes a roar of declaration that he is king! We too can discover that security to stand before people, not ashamed of the gospel. Each of us are able to walk with our head held high, confidently declaring that Christ is King. I believe that God is longing for the prophetic roar to be heard from His people once more. When this comes out of holy, righteous lives, those without Christ cannot help but take notice. We desperately need this bold and uncompromising nature that isn't put off by rejection or indifference, if we are to reach anyone for Christ.

2

The Potential of the Church in Evangelism

We live in tremendously exciting times. So much is happening so quickly. Even in our own lifetime we are seeing Bible prophecy fulfilled! The focus of world attention is constantly on the middle East. Across the globe there continues to be increased reports of wars and rumours of wars. On our television screens and in our daily papers we have frequent news of earthquakes, famines, and natural disasters. It seems that throughout the world there is unmistakable evidence that we are heading towards the climax of the end of the age. It is against this background of uncertainty, and in this atmosphere of anticipation, that God's people 'together' have a significant role to play in affecting society for Christ.

The Church should be the most powerful influence in the world and be proclaiming the most positive message in the universe. For much too long people have observed Christianity with indifference on the one hand, and laughter on the other. The common image that people have of Christians can be observed quite often in the media. Consider for example how you have seen the local vicar portrayed on television programmes. Either as a weak, goofy-toothed, bespectacled, doddery individual, someone who hasn't got it quite together; or as a pompous, legalistic hypocrite with a 'holier than thou' sort of attitude.

This image of Christianity is changing, the tide is beginning to turn. I believe we are coming to a time when God's people will no longer be observed with indifference or pointed to as an object of ridicule and humour. The Church will once again be held in respect and awe just as was the case in the book of Acts. It was then that we read the local community held the disciples in, *'high honour and more than ever believers were added to the Lord, multitudes both of men and women'* (Acts 5:13–14).

Over the last twenty eight years or so, through the 'charismatic movement', we have seen God move in a mighty way renewing the lives of many Christians. His Holy Spirit has been poured out and a major manifestation of His power through the gifts of the Spirit has been in evidence. He has brought countless thousands into a new freedom of praise and worship and has revealed to the Church in a clearer way, Jesus as Lord. Many wonderful truths which had been lost in the experience of Christians, are now being rediscovered.

God does not stand still though: He is moving on to fulfil His plan and divine purposes. There is always the great temptation to settle down secure in the blessing of our past, or even present experience. But the Lord is preparing His people today, getting them ready for what lies ahead. We are I believe, in the purpose of God, heading towards a great revival. By a sovereign move of God's power throughout our land, the Church will make a significant, noticeable impact on society once more.

Some people's understanding is that revival is being held back because of the heathen state and rebellious hearts of unconverted men and women. This couldn't be further from the truth. It is the present state of the Church that is the major blockage to revival in our nation. The proud, unbelieving, independent hearts of God's people is delaying all He wants to do. Judgement must first begin with the household of God. In Malachi 3:6–12 we see how God is just longing to open wide the windows of heaven.

His desire is to pour down upon us an overflowing blessing so great that we would not be able to contain it. The condition is that we His people repent of robbing Him and give willingly all that He expects of us.

God promises to move in our land and to bring about change but makes this conditional on a righteous response from His people,

> 'If my people who are called by my name humble themselves, and pray and seek my face, and turn from their wicked ways, then I will hear from heaven, and will forgive their sins and heal their land.'
>
> (2 Chronicles 7:14)

United We Stand

God is restoring to the Church many things, not least an understanding of what Jesus meant when He said, 'I will build my Church' (Matthew 16:18). Throughout the land God is bringing back to His people a greater awareness that the power of the risen Lord is to be released through the corporate, committed body of the Church. Together we are to stand as one, rather than separate, independent individuals trying to stand as the Church. He is bringing a deeper understanding that fellowship and committed relationships with one another are a vital part in that building programme. God says He will 'command the blessing, where brethren dwell together in unity' (Psalm 133:1 & 3). This has far greater implications than just in our own local congregation though of course this is where unity must begin. God is speaking to His people across the nation that we must move together as one, regardless of our denominational or non-denominational label.

For years that old battle hymn, 'Onward Christian soldiers marching as to war,' always used to be a source of much confusion to me. I would sing along with great gusto verses like, 'We are not divided, all one body we' and

'Like a mighty army moves the Church of God'. As I did so I couldn't help but think, when looking around me, where was the reality of this? In the past I wondered, was this an over enthusiastic, rather optimistic hymn writer, or had he seen something in his spirit that God's heart was expressing for us today? Now when I consider these words a sense of excitement and expectancy grips me. Today we are starting to see evidence of this move of God's people coming to fulfilment in our land.

The New Testament Church made such a powerful impact and experienced such a great anointing upon their witness because of their unity. We need to repent of our petty differences, pride, suspicions, and fear of one another and unite our efforts. Throughout the book of Acts we read that they were of *one heart, one mind and one spirit*. What we are talking about isn't ecumenical harmony, based on compromise; far from it. If we try to join everything together under the name of 'Christian' regardless of fundamental doctrine it will be fruitless. True unity can only be built on the foundation of truth, and established through our total commitment to Jesus Christ.

What God is looking for isn't everybody agreeing about everything, nor even everybody doing the same thing; this would only be dull uniformity. The important thing is each person working together, and seeing that the Kingdom of God being expressed through them, is of greater importance than their own prejudices and differences.

If we are to affect our community we should be first and foremost a working model of the Kingdom of God. That is, a gathering of united people through whom He can powerfully reach out to the lost and in whom His character can be seen. The Lord worked through His physical body two thousand years ago with great power and effect. Since His death and resurrection He is working through His spiritual Body the Church. God's people must come together as Philippians 1:27 describes to, *'stand firm in one spirit, with one mind, striving side by side for the faith of the gospel'*. Then there will be a release of power greater than we have ever known before.

When Christians are willing to pay the cost of putting Christ's Kingdom first and seek righteousness with God and each other, the potential of the Church will be fully realised. Then a clear, unmistakable message to those without Christ will be heard, and Romans 15:5 & 6 will become the reality that it should be in our experiences.

> *'May the God of steadfastness and encouragement grant you to live in such harmony with one another, in accord with Christ Jesus, that together you may with one voice glorify the God and Father of our Lord Jesus Christ.'*

We need to commit ourselves exclusively to the goal of living a Kingdom life based on the absolute authority of God's word. At the same time there needs to be an alertness to the bondage and division that theological convictions and doctrinal strongholds can bring us into. Our desire to please God and accept one another should become of utmost importance. Before God can dramatically change the area we live in we must first be willing for Him to change us, in our attitude and thinking towards each other.

Jesus said, *'By this all men will know that you are my disciples, if you have love for one another'* (John 13:35). We need to major on those things that we do agree on, rather than those things we don't! Paul's direction to the Church in Philippi was,

> *'complete my joy by being of the same mind, having the same love, being in full accord and of one mind. Do nothing from selfishness or conceit, but in humility count others better than yourselves. Let each of you look not only to His own interests, but also to the interests of others.'* (Philippians 2:2–4)

Some have a very negative attitude to this goal of God's people being united and would say that it is unrealistic and impossible. I want to say that it is absolutely possible for us to know this unity. We can believe for it on the basis that Jesus Christ Himself has faith for our being perfectly one. In John 17 He prayed four times, in verses 11, 21, 22 and 23, for this coming together, and we can be sure that His prayer will be answered.

God's perfect order is being restored in the Church, and the government of God will come into the world through a people who are committed to one another and are living under the rule and reign of King Jesus. This I believe, is going to culminate in a great revival! As the prophet of old foretold:

> *'For the earth will be filled with the knowledge of the glory of the Lord, as the waters cover the sea!'*
> (Habakkuk 2:14)

Revival is what we are heading for, a mass ingathering of people into the Kingdom of God on a scale such as we have never experienced before.

In revival you don't have to tell people 'they shouldn't do this and they mustn't do that'. Rules and regulations may help to set boundaries but in themselves never bring the dynamic life and power we need. It is a sense of God's presence gripping the heart of people that transforms lives. In past revivals we find that the statistics of rising crime, divorce, suicide, etc. start to fall. The pubs and discos close down. Pornographic and violent films become non-existent and the fear of God comes upon people bringing conviction even when there's not a preacher in sight!

'The Salt of the Earth'

The Church will begin to affect society as it rediscovers its tremendous potential as *'the salt of the earth'*. This starts when we get away from thinking of the Church as a building, the place to meet in, made of bricks and mortar. The Church is made of *'living stones'*, people being built together in relationships, something that stands to the world as evidence of a community that loves God, one another, and their neighbour as themselves.

Salt has many characteristics but probably one of the most relevant here is the ability to create a thirst in people. If there is any doubt about this, try a pinch of salt and see! Should you do so you would very quickly discover it having a dramatic effect. It would create within you a thirst for something, namely water! One grain of salt on its own could never do this, but a collective proportion of those grains has a drastic effect.

The life of one Christian is significant in its testimony and witness, but is nothing compared with the effect of the corporate Body of Christ living in unity and righteousness. Together we have the potential to create a thirst within the hearts of those in our society for New Life in Jesus. By exalting Christ in our lives we present to them the reality of a relationship with God that is alive, exciting and relevant to everyday life.

The full potential of salt can never be realised while it remains in the salt cellar. It was never intended to sit within a brightly coloured container on an attractively prepared table, beside a deliciously cooked dinner. For salt to be of any relevance and to serve its purpose, then it must be shaken out of the cellar and into the area of need. Together we should be out amongst people in a visible way in our community.

'The Light of the World'

Another figure of our corporate life together is of, *'a city set upon a hill'*. In the darkness its light cannot be hid, it is obvious to all. One lighted match held high in the darkness would be barely noticeable from a distance, but thousands of those matches placed together would easily be seen. Together we can shine in our actions, words and manner, reflecting the radiant character of God.

Light is able to reveal the true condition of things. Some years ago while working with the Open Air Mission, part of our evangelism would be to visit fair grounds at night and preach the gospel to the many passers-by. As all the excitement, flashing lights and the noise of the fair was going on all around us, we would be telling people about the love of God over loud speakers. The following morning I'd walk across that same area and be amazed at the dirt and litter scattered everywhere, even on the place where we had been previously standing. In the darkness this was not noticed but when the light came, it revealed the true picture.

As Christians, in our relationship to Christ the light of the world, we have the potential of being so completely different from the society around us. In our character and lifestyle, the unrighteous works of darkness should be exposed through the values we hold. The voice of the Church needs to be raised against social injustice, oppression of the poor and the many moral issues facing us today. Like light shining into darkness we can speak with a corporate voice together into these areas of need.

The positive side of this characteristic of light is that not only will unrighteousness be shown up, but also the alternative life that Christ brings will be seen. While standing at the fair ground in the dark I couldn't see the wonder of God's creation all around me. When the daylight came though, I saw the true picture of not just man made objects of entertainment, but the beauty of the fields, hills and trees nearby. They were there all the time, but hidden by the darkness.

In living righteous, loving, compassionate lives we can present to the world an attractive way of living. A lifestyle that is free from the taint of selfishness and sin under the reign of our glorious King. When this light shines into the darkness of society, the darkness has to go, just like turning on a light in a darkened room. The effect is very radical: the moment that switch is touched, no nook or cranny is left unaffected by the light, and the whole appearance of the room is totally transformed.

Motivation from the Leadership

The hour in which we live is a crucial time for Church leaders to be setting an example and motivating their members to be part of what God is doing. If those leading the Church do not have a united vision for evangelism, and have not prayerfully sought God for a definite strategy to affect their local area, then the Church will never reach its full potential and have the impact that it could.

Weak leadership is one of the major reasons for a church being irrelevant to the community and becoming cocooned in its own introverted interests. In some situations there is the problem of leaders who see evangelism as having a low priority. In others, they have no clear vision themselves of where they are going, and so just go round in circles never really getting anywhere. Then there are leaders who preach that evangelism is the responsibility of every member, but neglect to communicate in clear, practical, concrete terms how people are to do what has been said.

The key to achieving God's purpose for His Church is a leadership who have a definite vision. They know where they are going and how to motivate, equip and mobilise their people to follow. Clear vision and practical application will motivate the Church to move out in faith. *'Where there is no revelation, the people cast off restraint'* (Proverbs 29:18, NIV). To keep in step with God there must be a clear vision in our sights, and attainable goals to aim for. A Church that has no vision, or one that is blurred by no realistic goals being given, is an unruly Church. In effect everyone will be doing what is right in their own eyes.

31

The importance of each person having a clear vision is well illustrated if we consider a greyhound racing track. The hounds are all in their traps waiting for the starting gun. As the shot is fired the traps are opened. Out rush the hounds to chase a mechanical hare racing ahead of them around the track. The hounds run after the hare for all they are worth. With ears pinned back, tails tucked underneath their legs, and their bodies streamlined, they pursue the hare. The problem is this: some hounds run because they have seen the hare, but others run just because other hounds are running, and they get tired very quickly!

This is so true of many churches today. There are those Christians who have 'seen the hare'. They have a clear sight of their objective, they have seen the purposes of God in their vision and are motivated to whole-heartedly pursue them. But then there are those who are really just getting excited because others around them are excited. These people soon get discouraged and grow weary in their Christian race.

Each member of the congregation needs a personal revelation from God of the common vision for the church. They need an understanding of the part that they are to play and a commitment to see fulfilled what God has shown them. The responsibility of the leadership is initially to receive that overall vision from God and bring it into focus in their own minds. Then to communicate it to their members through practical teaching and a clearly defined strategy.

3

Preparing for Battle

If evangelism is to be effective, it is vital that the Church responds to God's call, not merely to 'embrace blessing' but also 'enlist for battle!' We need to be engaged in warfare on a spiritual dimension for those who are going to hear the Gospel if we are going to see any breakthrough in our area.

Spiritual warfare is at the very heart of effective evangelism. It is a militant advance in prayer, praise and proclamation, against the works of Satan. Evangelism without spiritual warfare is like an army going to battle with plastic weapons! That would be a ridiculous sight. Great energy and effort might be spent, but certainly no ground would be won. Instead there would be many casualties, with no real threat to the enemy at all, and defeat would be inevitable.

The reality of this battle is an aspect of evangelism that is not fully recognised by some of God's people today. Any evangelistic work that doesn't have spiritual warfare as a priority activity will find itself achieving very little. If we are going to think seriously about evangelism and how to affect our area, then we must take up the responsibility of this neglected ministry. Jesus said, *'No one can enter a strongman's house and plunder his goods, unless he first binds the strongman'* (Mark 3:27). As we consider this, there are four very important things that we need to bear in mind as soldiers for Christ.

Firstly, We Must Know Our Enemy

When an army goes to battle there is certain information that they want to know to give them an added advantage. Things such as: the likely strategy of the opposing force, their territory, weaknesses and strengths, etc. Probably the most important and obvious thing they need to establish is exactly who the enemy are. When the battle is raging and soldiers are not quite sure who it is they are fighting, the result could be disastrous. Shots would be fired at anything that moved. Casualties would certainly be high as soldiers found themselves shooting at their own men!

The Apostle Paul says,

> *'We are not contending against flesh and blood, but against the principalities, against the powers, against the world rulers of this present darkness, against the spiritual host of wickedness in the heavenly places.'*
>
> (Ephesians 6:12)

It is not 'people' we fight against in evangelism. Their indifference, apathy and rejection to what we say isn't primarily the problem. The battle must first be fought on an entirely different dimension.

In knowing our enemy we must be convinced that it's Satan's influence on people's lives that is preventing them coming to salvation.

> *'We know that we are of God, and the whole world is in the power of the evil one.'*　　　(1 John 5:19)

When we come across indifference or rejection to the Gospel it is because of the demonic power of God's enemy holding people back from responding to Christ. As people knowingly reject the rule and reign of Christ they open themselves to the kingdom of darkness whose ruler is Satan.

Our enemy is alive and his demonic agents are very real and active; they aren't a figment of our imagination. It is amazing the amount of unbelief that is evident in Christians as far as this reality is concerned. Theoretically, most would give mental assent to what the Bible says about the devil. However, in their practical daily living, prayer life, and approach to evangelism, many are far from believing.

The picture that often flashes into people's minds when thinking of the devil is of a red, horned creature, with a pitchfork and a tail. This is very dangerous because it is an image of humour that the world has given us and causes us to think less than seriously about our enemy. We must have a strong conviction that he is real and doesn't play games. In fact Satan has some very definite objectives that Jesus could see clearly: he has come to, *'steal, kill and destroy'* (John 10:10).

Our enemy is deadly serious, his heart is set totally against God and in direct opposition to evangelism. Paul could say, *'we are not ignorant of his designs'* (2 Corinthians 2:11). If only this were true for every Christian they would not find so much difficulty living a victorious Christian life and being fruitful in their witnessing. It is because of this ignorance, that Satan gains an advantage over people. They fail to see who ultimately is behind the division, lies, doubts, fears, besetting habits etc., all of which restrict people's lives today.

As Christians we need to be alert to the reality that Satan comes against the Church in basically two ways. Firstly, with subtle deception as *'angel of light'*, trying to lead people out of the will of God. Secondly, in strong defiance like a *'roaring lion'*, bringing fear and insecurity into the lives of men and women.

Perhaps you've heard some teaching that suggests Satan has no power, in fact that he is like a 'toothless lion'. What a foolish thought that is! This deception is easily exposed when you just look around both inside and out of the Church and see the evidence of broken, bruised and damaged people. Satan has immense power and can have a very strong influence over people, in three major areas:

(a) The Mind

'The god of this world has blinded the minds of the unbelievers, to keep them from seeing the light of the gospel of the glory of Christ, who is the likeness of God.'   (2 Corinthians 4:4)

I'm sure you've heard someone use the phrase, 'they've seen the light!' This is usually directed at new converts jokingly, by those who wish to mock, not realising the truth of their words. It is a fact that very often people are blind to what we are saying. They cannot see the judgement of God on their sin, and the beauty of Christ's love in wanting to save them.

As you share your faith with people it is common to hear responses like 'I can't see what you are getting at', or, 'I can't see why you get so excited'. With some people you can talk until you are blue in the face but to no avail. Satan has them bound by blinding their minds with things like materialism, intellectualism, and legalism. Even criticism, bitterness, immoral thoughts, pride etc., has a blinding effect upon people and can distort the way they see things. An old hymn expresses so well the power of the gospel to overcome this blindness.

'At the cross, at the cross
Where I first saw the light,
And the burden of my heart rolled away.
It was there by faith,
I received my sight
And now I am happy all the day.'

(b) The Spirit

We were created for the supernatural. There is that part of our being that longs for this dimension. If however, people reach out for a spiritual experience, without first coming to Christ in repentance and faith, they soon find themselves in bondage to Satan. With all the religious confusion in our society, and the explosion of interest in the occult and Eastern philosophies, this problem is very relevant. There is a great deal of curiosity about the supernatural today through films, TV programmes, books, games, medicine, New Age teaching, and witchcraft etc. Satan is using a whole variety of things that seem harmless, interesting and good, but ultimately bring oppression and bondage.

The increase of cults and sects in society is evidence of the deception that people are led into. It is said that seventy eight per cent of those involved in these different groups started out with a definite Christian foundation to their lives. Satan can capture the spirits of willing people. He can cause them to follow enthusiastically the deception that in many cases destroys themselves and the lives of their families. He is able to make things seem right to do but, underneath it all, the path leads to bondage.

(c) The Body

People can be oppressed and bound by the enemy through sickness. Of course not every sickness is a direct attack of Satan. There are some though who have given Satan a foothold into their lives through wrong attitudes, disobedience, compromise, dabbling with the occult etc. This can then manifest itself through sickness. In the gospels we read of people having a *'dumb spirit'*, a *'spirit of deafness'* and a *'spirit of blindness'*. In Luke 13:11 we find, *'a woman who had a spirit of infirmity for eighteen years'*. Then in verse 16 we see she was, *'bound by Satan'*.

Satan is so cunning that he can do more than bring a person into bondage through sickness. He is able to do the same ironically, through healing their sickness. One woman I spoke to shared with me that she'd got supernatural power to heal people. She only had to touch the part of their body that was sick and they would be made

37

well. On asking her what church she went to, I was told it was the local spiritualist meeting in the area. Nothing would persuade her that her power was not from God. She concluded that as it only did good to people, then there couldn't be anything wrong with it. Not only was she completely deceived but she was leading many others into deception as well.

Let us be clear, any healing power that comes to a sick person, or to the healer, that doesn't come via the cross of Jesus Christ is ultimately evil. Although it appears to bring relief in the short term, eternal bondage will result. It will divert people away from the divinity and uniqueness of Jesus Christ. His death upon the Cross and resurrection will not be of utmost importance to them. Their miracles and supernatural manifestations will not speak of the problem of man's sin, a person's accountability to God, the need of repentance and the reality of a lost eternity.

Having established who our enemy is, we have, I believe, spent long enough talking about his power. If we are to know our enemy we must know and be fully convinced that he is totally and absolutely defeated through the cross of Christ! As far as the Christian is concerned, Satan can have no power over our life unless we give him a foothold through disobedience or compromise. The Bible says that Jesus,

> 'disarmed the principalities and powers and made a public example of them, triumphing over them in the cross.' (Colossians 2:15).

Can you imagine the confidence and renewed strength that an army would have if before-hand they knew the outcome of the battle? If they could see beyond any shadow of doubt that their enemy was already defeated before a single shot was fired, the victory would be easy! It is essential, in evangelism, that we don't listen to the bluff of Satan and get discouraged. We are to listen to the truth of God's word.

'For the Lord your God is He that goes with you, to fight for you against your enemies, to give you the victory.'   (Deuteronomy 20:4)

Secondly, We Must Have a Battle Mentality

Our 'mind set' in spiritual warfare is of great significance. Often this is one of the first areas that Satan tries to attack. We must settle in our minds that there is going to be a battle as we move into action with the gospel. Frontline evangelism will always attract frontline attack. Satan will oppose us. He will attack individuals and also try to divide the corporate Body. We are at war and Satan will be at work in subtle ways to weaken our faith and unity.

A vital key is, if we think we are a failure we will fail, if we think we can't do something we won't. But if we think we are, *'more than conquerors'* we will conquer. If we dwell upon the truth that *'we can do all things through Christ'*, we will do them! Our mind needs to be set on what God's word says; then our actions will also come into line. The Bible says of man, *'As he thinketh in his heart, so is he'* (Proverbs 23:7, AV).

There is the world of difference for a soldier between the assault course of the training ground and the real war. All the teaching, training, exercise and theory in the world is nothing compared to what it's actually like in battle. People learn and develop far more from practice than theory, even though the theory is very important. In the same way it is not enough merely to listen to teaching on the subject of spiritual warfare, we must get on and do it. It is no good preaching theory to the devil, only reality will count!

This picture of an army of soldiers called to battle is a theme running throughout the Scriptures. In 2 Timothy 2:3 & 4 we read, *'share in suffering as a good soldier of Christ Jesus. No soldier on service gets entangled in civilian pursuits, since his aim is to satisfy the one who enlisted him.'*

We see that a soldier expects suffering and hardship, he is prepared for lots of hard work, bruises and pain. It would be a very naive and immature soldier who went into battle not expecting to get dirty and bruised, or for there to be some hardship and suffering. Likewise, evangelism will involve some knocks. Perhaps the bruising of our ego and flattening of our pride, maybe the feeling of hurt through rejection as we present the message of Christ. The strength of our character will be seen in our ability to take the knocks and be steadfast in continuing on with the work.

We see also a soldier is single minded. *'No soldier gets entangled in civilian pursuits since his aim is to satisfy the one who enlisted him.'* When he goes to the front line of battle, he is not thinking about the likely football result of how Liverpool did in their match against West Ham. Nor is he over-concerned with how England are getting on in the test match against Australia. Soldiers have one mind that isn't cluttered by other things, a mind that is committed to winning the battle and seeing the defeat of the enemy. As a soldier of Christ we can only be effective if we have one aim, and one objective. We need to discipline ourselves not to become entangled with anything that isn't part of that objective.

We must think of ourselves as men and women of a fighting character if we are to make inroads into enemy territory. Matthew 11:12 (NIV) says,

'The Kingdom of heaven has been forcefully advancing, and forceful men lay hold of it.'

This word 'forceful' need not be a negative thing. We can think of the character of a forceful soldier in battle, in positive terms and recognise some distinctive characteristics. This same nature can be applied to our own lives in a righteous way. Men of violence are committed to their cause no matter what the cost. They are willing to lose their own lives if necessary. They are uncompromising, whole-hearted and they fight to win! This degree of commitment is important if we are to stand against the powers of darkness in prayer and be effective in evangelism.

Thirdly, We Must Be Fully Dressed with the Right Clothing

Imagine for a moment the sight of an army heading for the front line of battle wearing only dressing gowns, slippers, and hot water bottles tied around their necks! It would be a ridiculous sight wouldn't it? The enemy would be at an advantage from the start. Not only would they see these men were unprotected, they would also discern that they were not too serious about their intention of winning. You could guarantee which of the two would be defeated. If an army is not dressed for battle they would not stand much chance of victory.

This might sound like a ridiculous extreme, but the fact is that for many Christians today, they rise up in prayer for evangelism, clothed in nothing more than dressing gown and slippers. It is not surprising that the powers of darkness haven't been driven back by this show of commitment. The seriousness of the battle that we are talking about is summed up in one word, 'armour'. We need to take up the armour that God has made available and show our enemy that we mean business!

Ephesians 6:11–13 stresses twice the need to, *'put on the whole armour of God'*. It is no use having only one part of this clothing on, or all but one piece. Every part is vital for full protection. We can be sure that the very place we leave unprotected in our life, will become our weak spot and would not go unnoticed by Satan. Before long those fiery darts would find their way to bring defeat into our lives.

Notice also that we are not born with the armour of God on. Nor when we became Christians did we automatically find ourselves wearing it. The scripture says, *'put on'* or, *'take the whole armour of God'*. The responsibility is ours. A conscious act of our will is needed, to take in prayer what God has provided and make it our experience by faith. In verses 14–17 of Ephesians 6 we find the different parts of this armour that we need be clothed with in battle.

(a) 'The Belt of Truth'

This speaks very much about reality and sincerity being at the centre of our life. Of being gripped and strengthened by the truth of God's word. Think of a competitive weight lifter preparing to lift very heavy weights. After chalking his hands with resin to stop them slipping he will walk over to the weight. Before he bends to lift it, he will take hold of the big belt around his stomach, take a deep breath and hoist it in another three or four notches. Then he bends and lifts the weight. The reason for this is the gripping action of the belt helps him take the strain of the heavy weight, so he doesn't damage himself. The same is true with ourselves; as we grip God's word, then God's word grips us. It becomes close around us and holds us firm as we take the strain of the battle.

(b) 'The Breastplate of Righteousness'

In service for God, especially in spiritual warfare, we need a heart that is clean before the Lord. A life of integrity and transparent honesty. Our lifestyle needs to be one of righteousness, completely blameless before God and man, giving no foothold to Satan. John Wesley once said, 'give me a hundred people who love God with all their hearts and hate nothing but evil and I will move the world!' Notice that it is a 'breastplate' of righteousness – this part of armour covers the heart. Holiness is something that must

42

come out of our hearts. We live righteously not out of a slavish sense of duty or because of a fear of being found out, but because there is no longer a love for sinning within us, only a willing delight to do what pleases God.

(c) 'Having Feet Shod with the Gospel of Peace'

This speaks of a communication of peace and wholeness in our daily walk. As servants of God we walk with a new sense of direction and authority. We walk in the truth and experience of what we are preaching about. Wherever we go we bring God's peace into situations. This experience of peace is something that people everywhere are searching for. It is though, for them, as elusive as trying to catch the wind. True peace is found when people know inside that they have been made right with God. As ambassadors for Christ, we need to be willing to use our feet and to walk, directed by the Holy Spirit to others. In love we beseech them on behalf of Christ, 'to be reconciled to God'.

(d) 'The Shield of Faith'

With this we can quench all the fiery darts of the evil one. This is an action of trust in God. It speaks about a life of trust and can only come out of our close relationship with the Lord. The battle gets tough at times and we can feel things are not going the way they should. Satan can whisper, 'you've failed', 'you'll never amount to anything', 'God doesn't really care about you'. The only way these lies and seeds of doubt can be stopped is by raising our heart in faith. Confessing in reality to ourselves, our circumstances and our enemy, that our trust is in the Lord. The key to effectiveness in warfare is the strength of our relationship with God. This is why Paul says, 'be strong in the Lord and in the strength of His might' (Ephesians 6:10).

(e) 'The Helmet of Salvation'

As we are dwelling upon what salvation has accomplished we have a renewed mind that is pure, positive and protected by deliberate intention. We remind ourselves of the fact that Satan and all his demonic powers have been defeated. Through salvation we have been given all the ability and resources of heaven that we need to serve God. The area of our minds can be a major battle-ground. Unless we are protected there, our whole life could just collapse. This is why God's word in Romans 12:2 says,

> 'Do not be conformed to this world but be transformed by the renewal of your mind.'

We need to meditate on what we've been saved from and how we are to live in this ungodly world.

(f) 'The Sword of the Spirit'

This is not, as often we've been led to believe, just the Bible. The Greek word is not *'logos'* meaning the whole of God's written word, but *'rhema'* meaning a specific word quickened to our spirit for a particular situation. W.E. Vine says in his book on New Testament words,

> 'Here the reference isn't to the whole Bible as such, but to the individual scripture which the spirit brings to our remembrance for use at the appropriate time, a prerequisite being the regular storing of the mind with scripture.'

So the sword of the Spirit is a specific word for a specific situation. The Word of God, anointed by the Holy Spirit and quickened to us to meet the need as we stand in warfare.

It's worth noting that the sword is drawn from the belt of truth, God's Word. This sword is the reality of God's Word active in our life. A good example is found in Matthew 4:4 when Jesus was being tempted by the devil. He simply turned round to him and said, *'It is written...'* and used the sword of the Spirit to defeat Satan. Jesus didn't just quote Scripture at the devil but spoke God's Word to His enemy in the power of the Holy Spirit.

Fourthly, We Must Be Fully Equipped with Appropriate Weapons

The weapons we use against our enemy are not guns, bombs, bullets and tanks – they would be most inappropriate. Because our battle is a spiritual one only spiritual weapons will be effective. That might sound obvious but some years ago a group of 'Christians' in America were buying up all the guns and tanks that they could get their hands on. It was their serious intention to be the army of God in the last days and to rise up against all the evil around them!

We have far more at our disposal than the sword of the spirit to drive back the powers of darkness and see captives set free. The Bible says,

> *'For though we live in the world we are not carrying on a worldly war, for the weapons of our warfare are not worldly but have divine power to destroy strongholds.'*
> (2 Corinthians 10:3–4)

These weapons which are so effective against the works of Satan are:

(a) Prayer

This could well be called our 'intercontinental ballistic missile'. It can reach anywhere at any time. Matthew 16:19 says, *'whatever you bind on earth shall be bound in heaven, and whatever you loose on earth shall be loosed in heaven'*. We have been given all authority by God to proclaim the Gospel of Christ. As we pray under authority we are able to bind the powers of darkness and loosen people to be able to respond to this message.

45

(b) The Name of Jesus

There is power in the Name of Jesus! In Mark 16:17 Jesus said, *'In my name they will cast out demons'*. Later on we'll be looking at the ministry of deliverance in evangelism but let us be reminded in preparation for battle that, *'he who is in you is greater than he who is in the world'*. We see in 1 Samuel 17:45 how David came against the demonically inspired enemy of God's people, Goliath. He said, *'you come to me with a sword and with a spear and with a javelin; but I come to you in the Name of the Lord of hosts, the God of the armies of Israel, whom you have defied'*. As David came in the power of that Name Goliath had to fall, he didn't stand a chance!

The hymn writer penned the words:

> 'Jesus the name High over all,
> In hell and earth and sky.
> Angels and men before it fall
> and devils fear and fly.'

(c) Praise

This is a major key to unlocking the doors of bondage and seeing God bringing a breakthrough. It is a very powerful weapon because *'God inhabits the praises of His people'*. The walls of Jericho fell to the shout of praise. Armies were defeated as singers and dancers went ahead of the warriors at the command of Jehoshaphat the King of Judah. Jonah was released from his captivity in the belly of the whale when he gave thanks to God. Paul was set free from prison and other prisoners came out of their bondage when at midnight they began to praise the Lord.

(d) The Blood of Jesus

In Revelation 12:11 where it speaks about our victory over the enemy, God's Word says here that His people, *'conquered him by the blood of the Lamb and by the word of their testimony'*. We are blood-bought children of God and as we stay righteous through the blood of Jesus, there is a place of safety. Because of what Jesus did on the cross we are in a blood covenant with God. This means that Father, Son and Holy Spirit, plus all the hosts of heaven will fight on our behalf against the enemy. Victory is ours because there is power in the blood of Jesus and it reminds Satan, together with all the demonic realm, of their total and complete defeat. The power of the blood is released against Satan who would seek to condemn us and intimidate us as we speak out our faith in its power. We can declare to the enemy, 'I am cleansed and you are conquered'.

(e) The Word of Our Testimony

In Revelation 12:11 we are told that it isn't just the blood of the Lamb that brings defeat to Satan, it's our personal testimony, the declaration of who Jesus is to us. Jesus Christ is Lord, the sovereign, almighty God! Whatever the circumstances, no matter how big the difficulty, we can declare the Lordship of Jesus Christ into every problem. We can confess our faith that, because God is still on the throne, *'all things will work together for the good'*. It is our personal faith that has such power, not just in who Jesus was, or will be, but who we believe Him to be right now!

(f) The Gifts of the Holy Spirit

We need the equipment of heaven to be fully effective for God. This dimension of the supernatural is essential, particularly the word of knowledge, word of wisdom, discerning of spirits, and the gifts of prophecy. The footholds that Satan has established in people's lives through damaging experiences in childhood, occult involvement, rejection, sin, failure, etc., can be exposed and pulled down. The gifts of the Holy Spirit speak right to the root of the problem and bring release. With this insight of spiritual knowledge we become more effective in praying against the enemy.

4

From House to House

A cold, windy day faced me as I went from house to house on the Northfield estate in Birmingham. I'd started out that morning with great enthusiasm to share the gospel but it wasn't long before my hopes were dashed. Nobody had any interest at all in listening to what I had to say. The damp, chilling wind only added to people's reluctance to stand talking at the door. Towards the end of that morning I remember calling out to God in prayer, 'Lord lead me to one person so I can honestly say that today has been worth while – please!' Having prayed, I went away to have lunch and pondered on the disappointment of the morning.

The first door I knocked on that afternoon was opened by a woman in her late thirties. When she realised I was from the local church, there immediately flashed a light of response in her eyes. As we talked, I heard how some ten years ago she had made a sincere commitment to the Lord. Since that time however, she had backslidden badly through involvement with a married man, while being already married herself. This relationship had broken up and she'd tried to commit suicide by taking an overdose of tablets. A short stay in a psychiatric hospital had followed and then, on coming out, there was I on her doorstep talking about Christ!

She looked at me with a hollow empty face and said,

'I've not known any joy or peace for a long time'. As we shared together, a miracle happened! God just dropped into my heart the words, 'read to her Isaiah 55'. This was so clear that I immediately got out my Bible and read the whole chapter. Then God impressed upon me to point out verse 6 so I read, *'seek the Lord while He may be found, call upon Him while He is near; let the wicked forsake his way, and the unrighteous man his thoughts; let him return to the Lord, that He may have mercy on him, and to our God, for He will abundantly pardon'*. I was then prompted to show her verse 12, this said, *'for you shall go out in joy, and be led forth in peace'*.

When I'd finished reading these words she became very excited. Tears started to fill her eyes and she said, 'you'll never believe this; I was reading my Bible only this morning and I've not done that for at least ten years. As I read, two verses seemed to leap out from the pages at me and I underlined them!' Excitedly she rushed to get her Bible and opened it to Isaiah 55. There before my very eyes, underlined in black ink that same morning, were the two verses I had just mentioned! As you can imagine, this amazing event not only changed the woman's life, as she repented and recommited herself to God, it also transformed mine! The incident restored my confidence in the worth of door to door witnessing, and I've never doubted its value since.

I believe this type of outreach is without question one of the most effective forms of planned evangelism. It is an aspect of witnessing that I've been engaged in throughout the country for over fifteen years now, and one that I can definitely commend to every church. Very often the fruitfulness of this work is seen only in the long term as it is primarily a sowing ministry but, praise God, times of reaping will come! While there will be a mixed reception, the right person calling at the right time, with the right message will certainly be used by God.

The Aims of Visitation

We should have specific goals for anything that we do if we are going to achieve what we set out for. If we aim at nothing the devil will make sure we score a bulls-eye! Having specific goals gives us something to pray and work towards in more concrete terms. The four major aims I believe in visitation should be:

Firstly, to *Discover* the needs of those people around us so that we understand where they're at and what problems they are burdened by. This enables the church to 'scratch where people are actually itching' and be relevant in a community. In being able to identify with those who are hurting, confused, fearful etc., we can begin to build bridges, gain people's trust and establish greater credibility in an area.

Secondly, to *Demonstrate* the church's love and interest and to care practically. We want people to know that the gospel is more than just words. As someone once said, 'people will judge you by your actions and not your intentions – you might have a heart of gold, but so does a hard boiled egg!' In discovering the needs of those we visit there will come opportunities to help people who are struggling and to get involved in some of the social problems which arise. This might include offering to do some gardening or the shopping for an elderly person. Perhaps making arrangements for a baby sitter for a one parent mum under pressure, who needs to get out. Maybe offering to visit a sick relative who is in hospital, or a person's friend in prison.

Thirdly, to *Declare* in a gentle, sensitive and appropriate way, the 'good news' that Jesus is the answer to every need of mankind. The gospel is not just about the forgiveness of sin and being reconciled to God, wonderful though that is. It is able to bring wholeness into a person's life and meet their deepest emotional, psychological and physical needs as well.

Fourthly, to *Distinguish* who the open and interested

contacts are so that these can be followed up and concentrated on. This is one of the exciting things about visitation. While many might show little response to what we're saying, there will be those who are searching and do want to know more. It is through careful, systematic visitation of an area that sooner or later we will eventually come across these people.

Preparing to Go Out

1. As we get involved with door to door visitation it is essential that we make sure we are moving out in faith. Just embarking on a bright idea or merely perhaps because we feel we ought to, will be no good at all. We need to be motivated by faith and believe in what we're doing. *'Faith cometh by hearing, and hearing by the word of God'* (Romans 10:17, AV). The biblical basis for our visitation is found in Acts 20:20. Paul not only preached in public but went from *'house to house'*, sharing the gospel.

Although some say that visitation is old fashioned, the fact remains that this form of evangelism is still very effective today. Consider for example, how much faith people like the JW's, Mormons, and salesman have for this activity. Even politicians, although they can promote their policies through TV, radio and the newspapers, know only too well that nothing can beat the one-to-one conversation on the doorstep! As an election approaches out they'll be, come rain or shine, whatever the weather, going from house to house.

2. A well thought out and carefully planned strategy is more likely to meet with success than haphazard visiting. This takes time and prayer and should be given top priority. Prayerfully choose the streets that you will concentrate on, being careful not to take on too large an area at one time. Praying about the estate, particular roads and even specific houses will be an important part of the preparation.

3. While it is true to say that the best training ground for people is 'on the job' and more is probably learnt in the actual 'doing', than in talking, some instruction should be given. This needs to include practical teaching on the kind of approach to make when knocking on someone's door, how to answer difficult questions that could arise, and how to lead someone to Christ. Great benefit will also be gained by encouraging people to read helpful books, watch videos or listen to relevant tapes on personal evangelism.

4. One very effective way of minimising rejection before you actually knock on a person's door, is to deliver a pre-visitation letter on church-headed paper. This should be delivered a week prior to calling, and the content would introduce the church and mention its desire to be more relevant to the community. It would then say that two authorised visitors would be calling with a questionnaire to enable the church to be aware of people's needs, and to establish how best they can serve the estate. The letter should reassure the householder that the questionnaire will be anonymous and only take a short time to go through.

There are two advantages of adopting this method. Firstly, advance notice is given of the visit and, secondly, it has the 'can you help us approach'. This normally causes people to feel less threatened and helps lower some of the barriers that they would normally raise.

5. It would be helpful for those visiting to read all the literature that will be given out so that everyone is familiar with what they are offering to others. This should be stamped with the church's address and telephone number to give people who receive it the opportunity to make contact if they wish.

6. A notebook and pen will be needed to keep a record of each visit and a small pocket Bible will be useful. Always try to avoid carrying a large Bible. Not only is it cumbersome, but it can be a little off-putting for those who see you coming.

7. It would be good to try and involve as many of the church as possible in the witness. There will be some, however, who feel that they are unable to go out, perhaps the elderly or those with some disability. These people should be encouraged to still feel an important part of the outreach, as prayer back-up, whether in the church or someone's home.

8. It would be wise at first to keep the visitation time to about an hour, so that the outreach doesn't become a burden to anyone. Have in mind also a specific time when people could come together afterwards. This would give opportunity for mutual encouragement as they share together the positive contacts that have been made. I remember very clearly an incident during a crusade at Oxford that bears out the need of this point. One young lady on our team had come back from the morning's visitation very discouraged, in fact quite upset. Although other people had experienced many good contacts, as far as she was concerned there had only been rejection. Realising she was at the point of giving up, we prayed and encouraged her in what God could do and asked the Lord to bless her as she went out in the afternoon. On returning a few hours later she was a changed person. Not only had there been worthwhile contacts but she had led two people to Christ!

Some Practical 'Do's' On the Doors

1. When visiting in a systematic way around an estate it is important to keep a clear printed record of every house that you are going to. A simple key to write down alongside the number of the house could be: A = out, B = slight interest, C = very interested and worth a re-visit. For those who are open and another visit would be worthwhile, then some additional information would be useful, i.e. the person's sex, approximate age and response, and their first name if they are happy to give it.

2. Visitation should always be two by two where possible. This is a scriptural principle but is also very practical. Being with someone else has the benefit of bringing greater security and confidence to each individual and of reinforcing their testimony. It also enables you to pray for one another while conversations are taking place.

3. As difficult as it might seem, try to relax and be natural. If we are uptight and anxious then we will sow that feeling into the other person. There is only one way we can truly relax and that is when our confidence is totally in God. The burden is released to Him and we accept that the whole weight of responsibility is not ours but God's.

4. Right from the start, we must realise the need to break down the barriers of suspicion and fear. People automatically raise these when they see two strangers walking down their path and knocking on their door. A simple smile and friendly manner expressing warmth is a major key. Just a cheery greeting can go a long way to help lower these barriers. C.H. Spurgeon when speaking to his students on this point of friendliness once said, 'An individual who has no friendliness about him had better become an undertaker and bury the dead for he will never succeed in influencing the living!'

5. In your opening sentence it is necessary to get across basically three things:
(a) who you are,
(b) where you're from, and
(c) what you want.
This opening sentence is the most crucial. The opportunity will be won or lost by how the conversation is begun. Often it will be helpful to say right at the start that you are not a JW or a Mormon, to allay fears. This might become a little embarrassing if you unknowingly happen to be speaking to a JW or Mormon but, nevertheless, it is still necessary to keep in mind.

6. If you should happen to meet a spiritualist or someone from one of the cults, it is always worth sharing with them, but only up to the point where they are prepared to receive what you are saying. Much wisdom is needed here so that you don't let the enemy waste your time and keep you from other people who would be more responsive.

7. Go on to develop the conversation on spiritual matters by using open-ended questions (who, where, what, why, how, when?). Take care though, of not giving the impression that you're interrogating them. The right questions are so important as they can really unlock the whole conversation. Jesus was certainly the master communicator, particularly in this respect and a good example for us to follow. Throughout the four gospels we see recorded over a hundred questions that He used to open up situations; for example Mark 5:30, John 8:10, John 20:15 etc.

8. Always try to bring the conversation to a positive conclusion. One helpful way to do this is to ask, 'having heard all that I've said about God's great love for you, can you think of any reason why you shouldn't accept Jesus Christ right now?' To put it in these terms helps the person to consider what it is that is holding them back.

9. Using the gifts of the Holy Spirit can make a powerful impact on people. God I believe will give discernment, words of wisdom and knowledge, words of prophecy, etc., that are beyond our natural ability, if we ask Him to. This will bring a greater awareness of God's presence to help touch their hearts. With those who are responsive and open we should be alert to the possibility of praying with them. While we must be sensitive about this, we should never let embarrassment hold us back.

10. Have the goal to always leave the person with a good impression, and thank them for the time they've given you. Even if they've been rude or shown little interest, offer them some relevant literature and a warm invitation to the church.

11. Sometimes you will meet a person who goes to church and appears very good and religious, but you just have that witness in your spirit that they've never been born again. It is often helpful with these people to ask them, what they would say qualifies a person to get into heaven. Almost without exception they will come back to their good works and sincerity. This will then give you an opportunity to explain clearly why Jesus had to die and what it means to be, 'born again'. Your own testimony at this stage can also be a great help.

12. When covering an estate in a systematic way and on a regular basis, it's a good idea to take a note of houses that have just been sold. In doing so you will be able to make a visit on the new owners as soon as they move in. The new occupants would certainly remember someone who went out of their way to welcome them into the area on behalf of the local church. You could let them know the times of your meetings, especially of the Sunday school for their children. There would also be an opportunity to offer them any help or information on local amenities such as shopping centres, doctors, dentists, schools, bus services etc.

Some Practical 'Don't's' On the Doors

1. Never take someone's initial reaction of disinterest or rejection, as their final word. Often this is just part of their defence. Having said that, don't be too pushy either. We ought to speak with enthusiasm and confidence expecting them to be interested, but be careful of overdoing it.

2. Don't assume that the facts of the gospel are known. There is an amazing ignorance today regarding the Christian faith. Very often the facts have got distorted and confused with those of other religions, cults and sects etc. Take nothing for granted, establish where they are at and what they believe, then work from there.

3. Try not to use religious jargon. We need to keep what we are saying simple, without speaking down to the person. Even terms like 'sin', 'repentance', 'born again', 'believe', 'commitment' etc., need to be explained so that we are sure the people we are talking to mean the same things as we do.

4. Never just dismiss a person's views to impose your own. Be a good listener. When someone listens to us without interrupting, changing the subject or offering hasty advice, we know they really care. It's important to us. Listening is more than just staying silent while another does the talking. It is paying attention, showing interest and affirming the worth of their comments. As we listen we need to be sensitive to what the person is saying for good 'lead-ins'. In doing this we are trying to pick up any distortions and misconceptions they might have. Also we begin to discover the hurts and doubts that they battle with. As you listen, try to identify where you can with what they're saying, and appreciate the remarks they make. Let them talk but still guide the conversation in the direction that you feel God leading.

5. Don't provoke the person unnecessarily, by being too blunt and insensitive. Care needs to be taken that the conversation doesn't get heated and turn into an argument. Remember, *'A soft answer turns away wrath'* (Proverbs 15:1). Also the Scripture says,

> *'Always be prepared to give an answer to everyone who asks you to give the reason for the hope that you have. But do this with gentleness and respect.'*
> (1 Peter 3:15, NIV)

We could so easily win the argument but lose the person we are talking to, then nothing would be gained. Just like the surgeon who said, 'the operation was a success, but the patient died!'

6. Be careful not to get drawn out of your depth into 'intellectual gymnastics', or being taken off onto irrelevant issues. If you can't answer their question don't fob them off or get defensive. Be honest and say so, but offer to find out and come back to them at a later date.

7. Don't be too obvious when you're taking down notes. We must be wise in this so that we don't cause alarm or offence. It would be unhelpful to be writing things in a blatant way right outside the person's front window or worse still while you're standing on the door step talking to them! The exception to this of course is when you are using a questionnaire, but in that case they will understand what you are doing.

8. Don't overstay your welcome! If you do get invited in, be careful not to stay longer than the person is comfortable with. You might think you're having a wonderful time, but the person could be feeling, 'I wish they would go – how can I get rid of them?' A good contact could so easily be spoilt simply by staying too long.

9. Never pressurise anyone to make a commitment to Christ. We can only lead the person as far as the Holy Spirit has taken them. The person must be genuinely under conviction and at a place of true repentance for any real progress to be made.

Finally, I know that people approaching door-to-door work may get concerned and anxious as there's so much to think of. They often wonder how they are going to remember everything. We need to believe that having been diligent in our preparation and tried our best to take in all we can, that the Holy Spirit will bring to remembrance the right things for each individual we meet. Jesus spoke to His disciples regarding this, He said,

> *'Do not be anxious how you are to speak or what you are to say; for what you are to say will be given to you in that hour.'* (Matthew 10:19)

5

Evangelism in the High Street

'Some want to live within the sound of church or chapel bell, but I want to run a rescue shop within a yard of hell.' These were the words of C.T. Studd. He was an outstanding man of God who left his fame as an English cricketer, and a considerable fortune, to go out as a missionary with the gospel to China, India and Africa. His passion for those outside the Church burned like fire in his bones, and was the motivating force behind his commitment to sacrifice all for the sake of those outside the Church.

Why Should We Go Out Onto the Streets?

I believe this is an important question to answer so that we might be motivated by the practical as well as spiritual purpose in street evangelism. When we can see the good sense behind the activity it is more likely that we will move out with a greater degree of conviction. As someone once said, 'We will see God in our streets when we start to relate to the people in our streets. The onus is on us to make a vital change in our thinking and Church lifestyle'. I believe this is one of the major keys to seeing God's blessing released in an area. Let me give four reasons that may help answer the questions we are considering.

1. Just to stay in our church buildings is unscriptural. It's as simple and straightforward as that. Evangelism from the armchair or church pew was unimaginable in the

New Testament. Throughout Scripture we see that the gospel was shared on the sea shore, in the market place, on the hillside, at the street corner and from house to house. As we mentioned in an earlier chapter, our vision needs to be more than the, 'come and be saved' approach, where the gospel is shut into a 'special service'. If we want to see God reaching the people of our area we must accept He has chosen to do it through our lives. What God is able to do is linked to our willingness to be used, as the scripture says,

> 'Now to Him who by the power at work within us is able to do far more abundantly than all that we ask or think...' (Ephesians 3:20)

God's power should be demonstrated where it was always meant to be seen – out amongst the people where the needy are.

The biblical basis for evangelism has its emphasis on 'going' out, not waiting for people to 'come' in. Acts 17:17 shows us that Paul was a real opportunist:

> 'He argued in the synagogue with the Jews and the devout persons, and in the market place everyday with those who chanced to be there.'

Religious instruction was given inside God's house for those who were inclined towards the Scriptures but those that weren't, were reached out to where they were. In Acts 26:26 Paul could say about his commitment to reaching others, 'This was not done in a corner!'

2. Non-Christian people simply won't come in to our services in any great numbers. Unfortunately not too many will come banging at the church doors wanting to know what time our next meeting starts. We don't often see people falling down on their knees in the church car park crying out, 'what must I do to be saved?' To the ordinary person the image of Christianity has been distorted to give the impression of it being dull, boring and quite divorced from their personal problems. Often the experience they've had of religious meetings is so alien to anything that they've been used to that it's hard for them to relate to it. The Good News of God's love appears uninteresting and irrelevant to them.

3. There is no other place where you will find such a variety of people as in the High Stret; a wide cross-section of age, need, culture, class, nation and belief. More unconverted people can be contacted with the gospel in one day outside, than we're likely to see inside a church in five years. It's worth asking yourself how many non-Christians over the past twelve months you've seen in your own services. Then compare the figure to how many could be reached if the whole church went onto the street and made contact with those outside.

4. One other important reason for getting outside the 'fortress' of our building is the impact we can make on Satan's kingdom. Going out will be an opportunity to demonstrate to the powers of darkness over an area that the Church really is serious about reaching the lost. Through the declaration of public praise and preaching we proclaim the victory of Christ and the defeat of Satan, to the spiritual forces of evil. This is especially important to have in mind when, sometimes, we might see few people actually stopping to listen. It's on these occasions when perhaps we find ourselves tempted to think, 'what's the point of this? It seems a waste of time', that we need to bear in mind the spiritual battle we are engaged in.

Street Witnessing – A Revelation and an Education

A Revelation of Human Need

There is always the danger when we stay within the church of losing sight of the needs of those around us and therefore getting out of touch. We can become so introspective that people's difficulties remain outside our experience. Life today is hard for many and the emotional, psychological, social, physical and environmental struggles that people have, can go unnoticed. Right on our doorstep are those with relationship problems, and drug and drink related problems. People who are imprisoned by loneliness, fear, confusion and abuse, are all crying out to be helped. Jesus said, *'Lift up your eyes, and see how the fields are already white for harvest'* (John 4:35). The need of the human heart the world over is still the same and hasn't changed in two thousand years.

An Education in Human Behaviour

There will be a wide range of reactions and we'll certainly find that some people can be less than grateful for our concern. Let me just mention for example the type of responses that you'll come across. I know they exist because I've met them all in the course of street witnessing – fortunately not all on the same day – but they are out there! Firstly, there will be those who pretend they've not seen you, and look straight through you as though you don't exist. Then you'll find people who see you coming toward them and so give you a wide berth by crossing over the road to avoid you. You'll meet the indignant who sharply say they're O.K. and that they don't need Christianity! Then there's the comic who likes to poke fun at you and make you feel about an inch high. The religious who considers your zeal an embarrassment; and of course the intellectual who wants to wipe the floor with you, with his clever arguments.

The reason for mentioning these things is that we need to be very careful of becoming indifferent to the difficulties of those we meet. Also of reacting to negative responses from people in a wrong way. The right attitude of compassion will always be the key to our effectiveness. The story is told of a young Salvation Army officer who was sent abroad to the mission field into a very hard tribal area. After several years of fruitless ministry he wrote of his discouragement in a letter to General Booth. In receiving this letter and sensing the crushing despair of the young officer, General Booth immediately sent him back a telegram. It only had two words on, but what was written revolutionised the officer's life and ministry. Those two words were – 'try tears'!

This genuine love for people is something that we find throughout Scripture, in Psalm 126:6, Acts 20:19, 2 Corinthians 5:14 etc. As we look at the ministry of Jesus we read that, *'When He saw the crowds, He had compassion for them'* (Matthew 9:36). The shortest verse in the Bible speaks of the feeling of Jesus for the death of Lazarus. It simply says, *'Jesus wept'* (John 11:35). This is not something we can 'work up' ourselves. It is the result of being filled with the love of Christ and having a genuine concern for those we are trying to reach.

Three Things to be Aware of in Our Preparation

1. Fear is the Great Inhibitor

Proverbs 29:25 says, *'The fear of man lays a snare.'* The devil tries to shackle us with fear in all its complex forms, to hinder our evangelism. The effect of fear can subtly replace our enthusiasm for the lost with the 'holy huddle' syndrome. Even on those occasions when we do manage to go out we end up evangelising ourselves! In Acts 20:27 Paul could say, *'For I did not shrink from declaring to you the whole counsel of God.'* The temptation will always come for us to, 'shrink back' in fear and remain silent.

A whole range of anxious thoughts can inhibit people. For example, the fear of doing something that might be considered strange and out of place by the majority. Fear of making a fool of ourselves. The fear of being rejected, or of being unable to answer someone's questions. The fear of being seen by someone we know, and the fear of failure. All these can bind us and make us ineffective.

2. Faith is the Great Liberator

We have the ability to overcome anything that would try to restrict our life, *'this is the victory that overcomes the world, our faith'* (1 John 5:4). Faith is simply agreeing with God and is always expressed actively in the positive effect that it has upon our life. Jesus said, *'you will know the truth, and the truth will make you free'* (John 8:32). It is by knowing in our hearts, what God says in His word, that our life is transformed. The faith we have in what God can do for us and what He can do through us for others, releases us to a new place of freedom and confidence.

Recently I was speaking at a church in Newcastle on the subject of evangelism. During the question time afterwards you could feel the atmosphere of fear that people had towards outreach. Several began to be negative and express their nervousness by saying that they could never go onto the streets witnessing. Not only were they restricting themselves by their confessions, they were also influencing others. Faith can only liberate us if we really believe God's word over and above our fears.

We need to have an active faith that says, I *AM* what God says I *AM*, *'more than conquerors'* (Romans 8:37). I *HAVE* what God says I *HAVE*: *'In every way you were enriched in Him, with all speech and all knowledge – even as the testimony to Christ was confirmed among you so that you are not lacking in any spiritual gift'* (1 Corinthians 1:5–7), and I *CAN DO* what God says I *CAN DO*, namely, *'All things in Him who strengthens me'* (Philippians 4:13).

3. Freedom is the Great Communicator

When the first believers were filled with the Holy Spirit they became so liberated that onlookers thought they were drunk (Acts 2:13). A new freedom had transformed them. There was no self-consciousness, no inhibitions, fear had been banished. Instead they were so free from embarrassment that they started to take a firm and uncompromising stand. In Acts 4:13 we find that the freedom and confidence these disciples showed really communicated something to those watching. The authorities took note that while they were uneducated and common fishermen, their boldness was evidence that they had been with Jesus. This spontaneity and liberty communicates not only life, conviction and reality to those we meet, it also communicates Christ.

I'll never forget seeing a group of people from the exclusive Brethren church conducting an open air meeting in Cornwall. There they were with their dark sombre suits, big black Bibles and glum serious faces. They preached about the unspeakable joy of knowing Jesus and the wonderful difference He could make to people's lives, but their words were empty. It didn't surprise me to see the reaction of disinterest in the faces of those passing by. What these Christians were trying to communicate was seriously undermined by the fact that there appeared to be no freedom or joy in their own experience.

Our evangelism must not be rigidly tied to a structure or method, no matter how effective it has proved in the past. We should not be bound to a system but free to hear God for each moment and each need which confronts us. Freedom and sensitivity to the Holy Spirit are essential. This does not mean that 'anything goes', but it does mean that our only restriction is God's direction. We see this demonstrated in the life of Jesus in John 5:19,

> 'Truly, truly, I say to you, the Son can do nothing of His own accord, but only what He sees the Father doing; for whatever He does, that the Son does likewise.'

The Open Air Meeting and Witness

1. First of all we need to find the most appropriate venue where there is likely to be a reasonable number of people around. In choosing the site, if a public address system is being used, make sure that you will not be too close to any shops. The particular venue will to a large degree determine the type of meeting you wil be able to have. This needs to be prayerfully considered.

2. If permission for the witness is required then be sure you have arranged this well in advance. It is always best to get this in writing if it is needed and to have the relevant letter of authority on you in case it is requested by the police or shop keepers. Normally permission will not be necessary unless you are using a private area of land, or the local by-laws restrict open air preaching.

3. Bear in mind the need to be careful about causing an obstruction or a nuisance to others using the area. Aim always to cause no offence to those who are trading nearby. If you are asked to turn down the volume of the amplification and the request isn't unreasonable, this should be complied with.

4. A basic framework for the witness will be necessary, i.e. praise and worship, testimonies, drama, sketch board, interviews, reading from Scripture, ministry in song, preaching etc. However, don't treat the meeting like a structured church service. You will have to be flexible and adapt to the situation that may be constantly changing.

5. Try to bring along anything that is likely to attract people's attention. Brightly coloured banners with a clear message are ideal. Also, a good assortment of tambourines and a variety of musical instruments will add to the celebration sound and arouse interest.

6. A more effective impact will be made with the praise and worship if everyone singing looks enthusiastic. There's nothing worse than singing about God's love and declaring how thrilled we are with Jesus, with long expressionless faces. People need to sing as though they really mean it, and that what they're saying is the greatest thing in their life.

7. It is important during the event that everyone concentrates on what is happening, so that there is no distraction through chattering. The group should be supporting those taking part and praying for what is going on. The encouragement of someone saying 'Amen', or 'Hallelujah', can do wonders to spur on those giving their testimony or singing. As people do this they are affirming others in what they are saying and giving them the assurance that they are not out there alone, but rather every member is behind them.

8. At least two people need to be giving out leaflets all the way through the meeting, and engaging in conversation with those passing. This can be a very valuable and fruitful ministry if the people involved are sensitive and alert to the opportunities around them. Also if numbers permit, then it would be useful to have some of the group standing in front of the witness, as part of the crowd, to draw others to stop.

9. Encourage as many as possible to give their testimony and for them to do so in a clear and concise manner. It's helpful to get people to have a rough outline in their mind before they start. A good exercise to do if they have never given their testimony before, is simply to write it down so they can judge what needs to be included and what can be left out. This needn't actually be used when the person speaks, but it will at least help them to be clear about what they want to get across.

10. You will probably find with preaching, that ten minutes will be quite long enough. Obviously, if a crowd has gathered and people are listening, then this can be extended. Those speaking should aim to be relevant and topical. Try to use illustrations from your own experience and the things around you. This turns the message into something that lives. One useful tip is to look through a selection of tracts and see the structure and content of how they've presented the gospel. Visual aids can be an excellent attention-getter, holding people's interest as you speak: use imagination here and be creative.

11. Try to remember the important communication which comes from your expression, tone of voice and movements when you are speaking. Experts claim that only 7 per cent of communication flows through our words. 38 per cent is communicated by our tone of voice and 55 per cent is conveyed by non-verbal signals, sometimes called, 'body language'.

12. Don't be too concerned about hecklers. If they are not too much of a distraction then they can be a great help in attracting and holding a crowd. However, if they start getting out of hand and causing a hindrance to the witness, then something needs to be done. A couple from the group need to try and draw the person aside by engaging them in conversation. If this fails then simply bring the meeting to a close and continue witnessing on a one-to-one basis until they have moved on.

13. After the meeting is finished it will always be fruitful to spend some time going two by two, contacting those that have been listening, and people passing by. Look around for people who are not rushing about and who obviously have some time to spare. Those sitting on a bench, standing at a street corner, looking in a shop window, or waiting for a bus are good examples.

14. Don't let people's indifference or hostility discourage you. Be realistic about their reaction while remaining in faith for a breakthrough. The promise of God's Word is,

> *'And let us not grow weary in well-doing, for in due season we shall reap, if we do not lose heart.'*
>
> (Galatians 6:9)

15. Some literature to hand out will be very useful when trying to stop people. Also using a questionnaire can be helpful both for yourself and also the person you want to contact. This approach tends to be less intimidating for those you are stopping, and often people will be more prepared to give you some time.

16. A flexibility about the kind of approach that is made to people should be kept in mind. Sometimes you will be able to be direct, as you ask them what they think of Jesus Christ. On other occasions you'll find it more appropriate to take your time and be less confrontational. The illustration of Jesus in John 4 with the woman of Samaria is a good example. Jesus didn't immediately start talking about her sin. Firstly, He broke the ice by asking for a drink of water. Then, having caught her attention, He began to introduce a spiritual dimension, by speaking about spiritual water. When her interest had been aroused, Jesus then brought about a prophetic confrontation, as He used a 'word of knowledge' about her personal situation. This resulted in not only herself being converted, but also motivated her to run back and tell others in the city. The outcome being, *'many Samaritans from that city believed in Him because of the woman's testimony, "He told me all that I ever did"'* (verse 39).

6

How to Share Your Faith Without Being Religious

'I'm not religious – I'm a Christian!' Often we say this with a measure of pride and confidence as we try to share the gospel with others, but if only this were true. Our lives and testimony would be more convincing and of greater interest to those around us if this was really the case. To many non-Christians, especially our neighbours, work colleagues and unconverted relatives, one of the biggest problems that kills the interest of others in our faith, is the lifeless appearance of mere religion.

The Bible says, *'in the last days there will be those who are holding to a form of godliness although they have denied its power'* (2 Timothy 3:5, NASB). This verse sums up what mere religion is all about. 'An outward show that lacks the reality of God's life within it'. If we are to share our faith in a way that doesn't immediately turn people off the first step is;

Recognising the Problem

This can be difficult because most people are likely to see the point we're making as applying to others but certainly not to them. In fact they might be quite offended at the thought that there could be anything less than complete reality in their life. After all, it is so much easier to see the *'speck'* in another person's eye than the *'log'* in our own. Consider the following areas that could be merely the 'religious shell' hindering the dynamic power of God being seen in us.

(a) Religious Convictions and Traditions

Often these convictions come from man's rules regarding religion and develop into areas of legalism, coming before our personal commitment to Christ. Jesus spoke strongly against the religious people of His day. In fact some of His hardest words were against those who had a form of godliness but were bereft of its reality. He said to the Pharisees and Scribes, *'For the sake of your traditions, you have made void the word of God'* (Matthew 15:6).

About fifteen years ago on a bright warm day, while working with the Birmingham City Mission, I was out witnessing in the Bull Ring with a team of people. An older man who seemed also to be distributing some literature was nearby, so I approached him. We began to talk, but before I could say very much he abruptly cut across what I was saying to state that he was from the 'exclusive Brethren.' He then wanted to know whether I believed in watching television. I started to say that amongst the poor programmes, there was also much that was good. Immediately I was stopped in mid-flow and he said, 'Brother you are on the broad road going to hell!' This was followed up without a pause for breath with the question, 'What do you think about women wearing trousers?' I began to say that it didn't really concern me too much, when he jumped in again, saying there was no question about it, I was lost and going to hell!! In an attempt to gain some sort of credibility with him, I explained that I was working with the Birmingham City Mission and was a committed Christian, in 'full time' service. It made no difference whatsoever to him as he just continued to tell me that I was under God's judgement. This was the sort of message that he was passing on to the people all around.

74

During one crusade in Fife while working with evangelist Don Double, we were setting up our equipment preparing for the first meeting in a Church of Scotland building. As we were placing the microphones in a central position one of the Deacons, looking rather agitated, came to us saying that we couldn't put them in front of the communion table as this would be quite wrong. Then he noticed that we'd moved two of the large communion chairs which were on each side of the table, to make room for the loud speakers. This really upset him, and we were told in no uncertain terms that they would have to be put back immediately. By this time he was so upset that he went away to cool down a little. Meanwhile we began putting up the bookstall. After a considerable amount of work and when the last book was in place, the dreaded Deacon returned with perfect timing. He took one look at the bookstall and nearly exploded! This for him was the last straw. We were told that there was no way we could have this in the Church because it was the 'sanctuary'. So we had to take it all down and re-assemble it in an adjoining hall.

These incidents might seem to be extreme cases, but they illustrate the sort of attitude that can be found in the lives of many Christians. The reasons why we do or don't do certain things can be based more on our religious heritage, than the new life we have in Christ. Such things as no games or television on Sundays, tee-totalism, the particular form of dress that is acceptable to conform to the 'norm' for Sunday worship, AV prayers in a language totally different from everyday speech, and worship to a set predictable pattern every week.

There is certainly nothing wrong with these things in themselves, we are entitled to our own convictions. It is when we become so rigid about them, that we start to get legalistic. We try then to impose our particular interpretation of right and wrong upon others, resulting in the life of God's Spirit being quenched. Sometimes we can find ourselves majoring on minor issues, or to use a more biblical term, *'straining out a gnat and swallowing a camel'* (Matthew 23:24).

(b) The Meeting Mentality

The Meeting Mentality can appear very religious and super-spiritual, and yet do a lot of damage to the liberty and joy that we have in Christ. What I'm referring to is where our life is always busy with endless frenzied activity – on this committee and that committee, busy rushing everywhere in the 'work of the Lord'. So busy though, we haven't the time for prayer, for people, or for practising what we preach. The over-enthusiastic Christian wife always out at meetings who has an unconverted husband, is a good illustration. Her husband comes home from a long day at the office, to find the house a mess because she's been busy helping at the church's mother and toddlers group in the morning, and then out at the ladies meeting in the afternoon. He looks around for his wife, only to find a note on the table that the dinner's in the oven and she's gone to the evening Bible Study! That sort of outward show of religion which lacks practical reality is sure to do nothing but drive her husband further away from any interest in Christianity.

Sometimes this Meeting Mentality can be used as an escape from responsibilities we need to face. I knew a Christian minister like this. He was so busy with religious activity that he had no time to build any level of relationship with his congregation. He was always either just going out to a meeting or right in the middle of something that had to be done so that he couldn't stop. It was impossible to pin him down to talk through important issues that needed to be discussed, and too busy to meet on a regular basis with his fellow elders. His activity looked very spiritual and gave him a sense of importance but it was actually a cover up. Before long the problems in his life started to surface and the mask of pretence that he'd been wearing became obvious to all.

The pressure put upon the congregation by their leaders to be at every meeting can also be part of this and will be counter-productive. It can be such that people are made to feel that they are backsliding or even in rebellion if they are not attending all that is expected of them. Realistic commitment to the church and its activities is of course very important. However, the treadmill of feeling that you have to be at everything is damaging. It can be harmful both to the family unit, particularly when there are those within it who are unsaved, and also to the vitality of life within the individual Christian. The result invariably is that people begin to get meeting-centred rather than Christ-centred, and are robbed of their joy. Reality is then replaced by religious activity.

(c) Super-Spiritual Solemnity

Super-Spiritual Solemnity at some church services can be a real barrier to the outsider; it's like entering another world! The 'Holy Silence' where people are afraid even to cough, or are embarrassed about their children making any noise can be a problem. A solemn formal atmosphere that creates a nervousness of doing or saying the wrong thing is very unhelpful. The glum serious faces of the congregation can be like going into a dentist's waiting room with each person expecting to be the next one in! Look at the expressions in your church and ask yourself, 'am I being pressed into this mould as well?'

Some seem to move into another mode when they enter a church. The tone of their voice changes, their expression is altered and their language is transformed into another era. They seem to endure rather than enjoy the experience of worship. People can give the impression of doing their duty and fulfilling their religious obligations rather than being glad that they're in the 'House of God'. A famous philosopher once commented, 'I would believe in their salvation if they looked a little more like people who had been saved!'

(d) Denominational Loyalty

Christians in many places have succumbed to this subtle deception of 'party spirit'. In Corinth nearly two thousand years ago, there were those who had the attitude, *'I belong to Paul, or I belong to Apol'los, or I belong to Cephas'* (1 Corinthians 1:12). This same divisive spirit is encountered widely today. To some, their denomination can be of greater significance than the name of Jesus Christ; making a god out of our denomination causes a person to appear proud, legalistic and self-righteous.

A letter published recently in one of the Pentecostal magazines caught my attention and stood out very grimly. It was from a person who felt enraged that some churches from his particular denomination had changed their name. His own words of anger summed up the bondage of Denominational Loyalty that I'm referring to. He said, 'over the years people have lived and died for the name of my denomination and I am prepared to do so as well! Others though are exchanging the name of their church for something more modern!!' What bondage this is where people worship the structure rather than the Saviour. It is then that there slowly comes a religious cloak of darkness which is nothing other than death!

Even those who claim not to be in a denomination can soon find themselves bound by the same spirit. It begins as they choose to go only to their own camps and conferences, and listen only to their own particular stream of speakers. Before long they too talk about their fellowship or grouping as if it alone held the complete truth and their leaders, the 'clearest' revelation.

The bondage of a misdirected loyalty brings a religious spirit restricting the wonderful and exciting diversity within Christianity. This is a subtle demonic spirit that prevents us being effective as we seek to win others for Christ. The Bible portrays only the local and Universal Church of God's people. It's as we recognise and respect each other as believers and reject labels, that we can know a greater fruitfulness in sharing our faith.

Taking Steps to Improve our Appeal

If we are to express our faith without causing people to switch off, our life must be much more than a religious shell. We have to take some conscious, deliberate steps to improve our appeal.

1. Be Attractive, Not Awkward

To speak without awkwardness or feeling clumsy, isn't easy but, praise God, it's possible. The life of Christ within us, in itself, has that irresistible drawing power which causes people to sit up and take notice. It's only when 'we' get in the way with our own ideas, and struggle in the ability of the flesh, that it becomes so difficult. Simply be natural and let the Holy Spirit within do the convicting.

Some years ago an author illustrated how not to witness with a picture of a so-called Christian walking around a supermarket. He was wearing a dark rain coat with a hat pulled down over his ears and was furtively searching for someone to witness to. Suddenly he came across a poor unsuspecting woman looking at some of the goods. As he passed her, she made the comment, 'my goodness, things are so expensive aren't they?' His response was, 'yes madam, very expensive, but not nearly so expensive as spending eternity in Hell! Are you saved?' Well there's nothing attractive and winsome about that sort of approach. In fact it's very awkward and clumsy and sure to send that person running away as quickly as possible.

Naturalness in itself is attractive. To help us in this we first of all need to pray to be less intense. Since we are filled with the Holy Spirit we can trust God to move through our life in a way that will draw the attention of others to us. Jesus said, *'If any one thirsts, let him come to me and drink. He who believes in me, as the scripture has*

said, "*out of his heart shall flow rivers of living water*"'
(John 7:37–38). The ability isn't of ourselves to convert
anyone; it is God's Holy Spirit in us who does the work.
We can pray therefore that God will flow through us and
give the right words as the opportunities arise.

To be attractive, it's best not to use 'the language of
Zion'. The religious jargon that we're familiar with can be
Double Dutch to the person we're speaking to. If an
Electronics Technician was to speak to me about ohms,
frequency modulation, or impedance mismatch, I wouldn't
have a clue what he was talking about. In the same way, we
need to make sure that we are speaking in terms that are
clearly understood by those we are witnessing to.

We also need to be consistent in our interest and attitude towards those we relate to. Not one thing on Sunday
and something else the rest of the week. If people are
never quite sure what mood we're going to be in, they can
feel as though they are treading on eggshells, afraid of
what our reaction might be. A sense of awkwardness then
develops in how to relate. We need to be known not as
people who are moody, easily offended or prickly in
nature, but consistent regardless of what is said or happening around us.

One of the most helpful things that causes us to be
attractive is a sense of humour. Perhaps the most common
impression that people have of Christianity is that it is dull
and boring. This is very often picked up because there are
some very dull and boring Christians about! To be able to
laugh, particularly at ourselves and not be so serious is
important. Enjoying and expressing humour whether we
are at home, work, or in the church communicates an
attractiveness that says, 'Christianity is fun!' It's something that can enrich and bring joy to our life, in a society
that is quite depressing and full of problems.

2. Be Passionate, Not Passive

There isn't much passion in mere religion, and when there
is, it can be simply something that is self-centred and

intolerant of the feelings of others. A godly passion is always Christ-centred, and its overriding concern is the good of others. It was said of Jesus that, *'When the days drew near for Him to be received up, He set his face to go to Jerusalem'* (Luke 9:51). We need to be passionately committed to God's call upon our life and enthusiastic about what we believe, because it's the most marvellous message that this world has ever known. How can we remain passive with such a thrilling Gospel! Jeremiah could say, *'His word was in mine heart as a burning fire shut up in my bones'* (Jeremiah 20:9, AV).

We should enjoy sharing our faith, not because we think we ought to, but because of the truth of such a wonderful message; it is *'the power of God unto salvation!'* A genuine heart-felt passion that takes us beyond mere religion, reveals the life-changing reality of the Gospel. This was very much the case as an eighty two-year-old man came into one of the crusades that I was conducting at Dersingham in Norfolk. That first night he was wonderfully converted. The next day I went around to his home to follow him up. As we sat talking over a cup of tea I asked him what it was that had brought him to the place of conviction the night before. Expecting him to say, 'young man, it was the fine sermon you preached last night, I just had to respond'! I was quite surprised when he said that it was the lively praise and worship in the meeting – so different from the 'prepare to meet thy doom sort of atmosphere that you get in most churches!!'

We minister what we are. If we're religious, legalistic and bound by all sorts of tradition, people sense it straight away. The same is true if we're simply passive in what we believe. When we try and talk about our faith, this is all they notice, and of course they don't want it.

Now in making this point, we need to be careful of going over the top in our enthusiasm. Beware of being insensitive, especially if we have unsaved relatives, or those very close to us. There's nothing worse than getting carried away trying to 'pea shoot' verses of Scripture at them. The over-enthusiastic wife trying to win her husband by putting tracts under his pillow at night and in his cornflakes box at breakfast, might well be considered as 'overdoing it' a little. However, the point is clear: there needs to be a genuine joy and passion in our lives about what we believe.

3. Be Involved, Not Isolated

Our lives must never appear aloof and separate in any superior sense. We are set apart unto God, consecrated in holiness to Him but we must be very much amongst people. I don't believe God would have us as His witnesses like some isolated monastic groups. Nor has He called us to be separated from the world in some sort of convent. The clear word of God is to, *'Go into all the world and preach the gospel to the whole creation'* (Mark 16:15). As we follow the example of Jesus we see that He was not merely in the temple praying, but out amongst the people meeting their needs. Thus, we ought to be very much in the world though not of it.

One of the great mistakes some Christians make is once they are saved out of the world, they turn their back upon it. In doing so they find themselves struggling to identify with the people that are around them. We need to be involved in secular activities of recreation, so that others can see our interests are broader than Bible studies and prayer meetings. If we've got children at school, then a good goal could be to try to get on the board of parent governors where we could have a positive influence on our child's school. When help on a practical level is needed in the community, that's where the Christian Church should be seen. Also our voice as Christians ought to be heard in debates on the social needs around us, speaking out for human rights and into political issues.

When there are television or radio programmes that are offensive, we should take some action. Rather than grumbling to ourselves, we have every opportunity to speak out in a loving, gracious but clear way. There are also occasions when we can express ourselves in newspapers and magazines by writing letters or short articles. It's also a good thing to remember to write letters that are positive, expressing our appreciation for good quality programmes or services, and not just complaints.

4. Be Relevant, Not Ridiculous

There is no use wanting to be involved, aiming to have an influence that affects the lives of others as we speak, if we are not relevant in what we are saying. All that will happen is that we'll come across as some religious fanatic who is out of touch with the real situation. Because of this, if we're to be relevant we must be firstly in touch with God, so that we know what we believe and how best to communicate it. Then, secondly, we must be in touch with what is going on in society today.

That means keeping well informed with news events and current situations. Being aware of what is happening in the world of sport, music, the arts and with fashion etc. In doing so we can relate to people on the basis of the things that interest them and find some common ground. We are able then to speak to people where they're at, and in terms that show we know what we're talking about, and so have something relevant to contribute.

The attitude of the Apostle Paul is so helpful on this. He certainly was not a man of compromise but could say,

> 'I have become all things to all men, that I might by all means save some. I do it all for the sake of the gospel.'
> (1 Corinthians 9:22 & 23)

So that he might be relevant to those he was reaching, he made a conscious effort to share Christ from a place of identifying with where people were.

It's also a good thing to be constantly reassessing the type of meeting that we hold if we hope to be relevant to those around us. Sometimes we'll have to change the structure and form of our services and be flexible to accommodate those coming in. Perhaps a change of the time that we meet, even the day could be considered. Just because we've always met at 10.30 am on a Sunday morning and 6.30 pm in the evening doesn't necessarily mean it should always be so. The traditional Sunday School might be more appropriate on a mid-week night or Saturday. These are things that we need to bring to God in prayer that we might be confident that all we do is relevant and not ridiculous.

7

Friendship Evangelism

In 1936 a book was published in America that rocked the world. The author was an unknown YMCA instructor who left his job as a salesman to teach young people the principles of public speaking. His ideas were put into a book and became an immediate success. It stayed on the New York Times best sellers list for ten years, selling well over ten million copies! This book was called *How To Win Friends and Influence People*. The reason why so many were interested in this subject was simply because everybody needs a friend. Within us all is a deep need to be loved, accepted and to feel a sense of worth. For this reason friendship evangelism can be very effective as we seek to win others for Christ. Through this means of outreach a clear presentation of the reality of Jesus is experienced that people can relate to.

I can understand those who feel that perhaps door to door visitation or open air preaching is not their particular ministry. However one way that we can all be involved in winning others is through friendship evangelism. Following on from the last chapter, this is certainly one of the clearest ways we can share our faith without being religious. It can also be one of the most fruitful and lasting means of outreach that there is.

Jesus was called, *'a friend of tax collectors and sinners'* (Matthew 11:19), because He came alongside those who were scorned by the religious authorities. Their comment was intended as an insult and accusation but could hardly have been more accurate, nor paid Jesus a higher compliment.

When challenging the religious about their responsibility to the oppressed and needy, Jesus told a parable known the world over as, *'The Good Samaritan'* (Luke 10:30–37). Here we read of someone journeying down a dangerous road who was attacked, robbed and left for dead. Lying there bleeding and dying he was passed by as far as the religious were concerned. They ignored him and considered that he wasn't their business. But a Samaritan came along, the last person expected to offer any help, and he got involved. At the end of the parable Jesus brought the pointed challenge, *'Go and do likewise'* (v. 37).

We are expected to be like the good Samaritan to those on life's road all around us. There are people who have been bruised and beaten by their circumstances, those whom Satan has stolen something from, leaving them for dead. The Samaritan became a friend to the one in such desperate need. It is for us to take the initiative and begin to do *'likewise'*.

Firstly, *'When he saw him he had compassion'* (v. 33). In his approach to this person, the compassion he had came out of the fact that he 'looked'. We must see the depth of people's need and be moved with compassion for them. This is not something we can manufacture or pretend we have. It is the result of the love of Christ moving through us to those who are lost and without hope.

Secondly, we notice that, *'He came to where He was'* (v. 33). His compassion for the person who was in such an appalling condition did not let him go on his way, but caused him to come alongside. We cannot relate to those we're trying to reach from a distance. The ministry of Jesus was always to draw near. Just as Jesus came to where we were in leaving the glory of heaven, we too must leave the comfort zone of where we are, and come to meet people at their point of need.

Thirdly, His action was practical. He didn't preach a sermon at the man, or start to quiz him as to why he'd been so foolish as to travel alone down such a dangerous road. He poured in oil and wine, bound up his wounds, set him upon his own beast, took him to an inn and paid out money for his welfare, until the man was able to stand on his own two feet.

It is through this practical expression of friendship that the gospel becomes more than a vague concept; the Word becomes Flesh. This is not invading people's lives, but being prepared to show a genuine concern. It is being available to meet people's needs, even at personal cost to ourselves and drawing them into our lives.

As we look back at our own experience and listen to the experiences of others, we find that most people become Christians through the testimony and encouragement of someone they have learnt to trust. Our goals in friendship evangelism should be to win people's respect, build bridges of trust, and earn the right to be heard. We must never assume that we automatically have that right. It does need to be earned.

Starting the Friendship

Firstly, we begin by seeking God for who He wants us to specifically concentrate on and believe Him for. Those that He would have us especially channel our time, energy and faith into. We ought of course to have a general attitude of friendliness to all people. However, as we seek God for one or two particular people who we can focus on I believe He'll give us their names. It could be our next door neighbour or a colleague at work. Possibly someone that we just occasionally pass in the street or a fringe member of the church, but as we ask God where to start we can believe Him to show us.

Secondly, we need to be someone who is likeable. '*A man that hath friends must show himself to be friendly*' (Proverbs 18:24, AV). One of the most challenging things for us to face is the fact that people have got to like us, or at least be impressed by our life, before they will take much notice of what we say. I believe the old saying is very true, 'what you are, speaks a lot louder than what you say'. Sadly sometimes we contradict or undermine what we say by the attitudes and reactions of our life.

Thirdly, to help us start the friendship and take steps to be likeable people, we ought to consider how we can go out of our way to be helpful. This was brought home to me one morning while doing some gardening when we lived in Cornwall. I was cutting the grass and thinking how I could reach out to our next door neighbour who we rarely saw because of our travelling. God suddenly spoke to me, not in any audible voice but certainly just as clearly. He said, 'go and offer to cut your neighbour's grass as well.' I tried to dismiss this, thinking it was just myself, but the voice was persistent, 'go and offer to cut your neighbour's grass.' Eventually after some delay I plucked up the courage and knocked on their door. When it was answered by the woman I made my offer. She was a bit taken aback but seemed glad to let me get on with it.

After I had finished the work my neighbour came out clutching a bunch of flowers that she'd just cut from her back garden. Smiling she said, 'thank you so much, no one has ever offered to do that before. Would you like to take these for your wife?' As I took them and thanked her something was established in that gesture between us, and part of the bridge-building process with our neighbour had begun.

Now, it could be that in your situation, you could offer to do some shopping if you were going to the shops anyway, or perhaps give a lift into town to someone. Maybe as my wife often used to do with our neighbours, you could bring in the washing from the line if they were out and it started raining. Whatever it might be, it's just going out of our way to be helpful.

Fourthly, we need to use our imagination and be prepared for God to say some unusual things at times. Someone once said, 'McDonald's hamburger chain has got far more imagination to reach the masses than the average Christian has to reach the lost.' If we're honest we can probably see a lot of truth in this.

Using our imagination and expecting God to speak in unusual ways is well illustrated with what happened to a woman from Yonggi Cho's church in Seoul, Korea. (He has the world's largest church with a membership of over 750,000 strong.) This lady was very keen for evangelism and reaching her neighbours, but one day she was re-housed to a high rise block of flats. Anyone living in that sort of situation will appreciate that it can become like a prison. Once you've shut the door, you just don't meet or see anyone.

She became very frustrated wanting to reach out to her neighbours, so she prayed, 'Lord, show me how in this situation I can reach those around me.' Her prayer was answered in a very unusual way. He told her to ride up and down in the elevator for two hours every day! Can you imagine it, just up and down for two hours each day. It sounds ridiculous, but as she responded in obedience she started to meet her neighbours and got on first name terms. She'd help them to the door with their shopping and discovered the names of their children. Then after a while she invited them all round to her house for a meeting, and in this way some of them were won to Christ!

Being creative in how our home might be used to make contacts would be a good start. Perhaps just beginning on the basic level of inviting one person around for a coffee and chat. Then moving on to having different events in the home with a non 'religious' content that a group of people could come to. Maybe a Tupperware or Pippadee party. A cheese and wine party, books or toys party etc., the object being to gather a group of people in your home so they can get to know you, and for them to see that you're a likeable friendly, ordinary person.

Having established some degree of friendship, this could be developed further by holding a special Christian emphasis afternoon or evening. Through slides, video or a simple discussion of the Bible, there would be opportunity to clearly, yet sensitively share Christ with those you've gone out of your way to develop a friendship with. Perhaps even a special lunch with an invited speaker could start something quite interesting.

Fifthly, in starting the friendship we need to see the importance of being considerate and long-suffering particularly with those we don't find it easy to get on with. Especially with people like our next door neighbours. I've known people fall out over the volume of the hi-fi, or the noise of the children, the balls coming across the fence and even the way that the car has been parked outside their house. God puts a great responsibility on ourselves not to let things like this spoil the opportunity of friendship. The Bible says, *'If possible, so far as it depends on you, live peaceably with all'* (Romans 12:18). What a challenge!

When we first moved into our home in Cornwall, everyone in the street knew that we were Christians. This was because we used the Good News Crusade lorry to move all our furniture. In large bright orange letters on one side of the van were the words, 'Jesus is Alive Today' and on the other side, in even larger white letters was written, 'Good News Crusade'. So as you can imagine we were marked people!

Now there was one man directly across the street from us who didn't get on with many in the area and certainly when he saw me he was cold and indifferent and wouldn't speak a word. However, one day he had to have some building work on his roof and he needed some scaffolding erected up the side of his house. The problem was that we parked our car right beside his house in an official parking lot which we paid for.

One evening his wife came knocking on the door and asked if it might be possible to move our car for the building work. Without hesitation I said I'd be glad to move the car, thinking it would only be for a few days. 'How long do you want us to move it for?' I said. 'Two weeks' was the reply! Immediately I told her that would be no problem and we'd gladly move it. She went back a little surprised and the following day as I was walking down the street to the local paper shop, her husband appeared. He came straight across to me smiling and chatting away. Although he didn't mention anything about our moving the car, there was definitely a bridge built between us even though at one time he was quite hostile.

Strengthening the Friendship

Firstly, if we are to develop the friendship, we need to take a positive interest in them. You can make more friends in two months by becoming interested in other people than you can in two years trying to get other people interested in YOU. Without being intrusive we can show a genuine interest in the welfare of their children and progress of their work at school. Also showing an interest in their partner's life and hobbies is a good way to strengthen that bond of friendship. Remembering birthdays, and of course the simple Christmas card.

Inviting them around for a meal can go a long way to developing that friendship. The meal table is to do with far more than just eating. Over a meal we relax, barriers are lowered and those we've invited can see that we're normal people and not quite as strange as at first they thought. They also see that we haven't got to be always talking about church or quoting scriptures, but can talk naturally about the everyday things of life.

Secondly, we need to see our commitment as long term, so that we don't give up at the initial disappointments and set-backs. When someone doesn't immediately come to

Christ we need to continue in faith and not just write them off. A consistent demonstration of our love is important. 'A friend loves at all times' (Proverbs 17:17). There will be times when we might feel let down by something they've done or a promise they've not kept. That's the very nature of any relationship. Because of this don't expect perfection from the friendship. We must be prepared to be vulnerable and at times we will be hurt. This is when we need to remember the patience, forgiveness and love of Christ towards us and continue to reach out with His supernatural grace.

An illustration of this principle of long term commitment can be seen in an example I heard, about a missionary couple who had been sent out by their church to some villages in India. After three years the couple came home on furlough and in their report to the church they shared that there had been no converts yet, no church services started and no significant contacts made. Their home fellowship were surprised by this but didn't say anything to the couple. They encouraged them and prayed, sending them back again to India.

Three years later, after six years, they returned and the report this time was a bit brighter. Still no converts had been seen, but they'd made a number of good contacts and were starting to get a better grasp of the language and culture of the people. Well it wasn't very positive, and by now the church wondered if the couple had backslidden. Nothing was said to them but they prayed over the couple again and encouraged them as they returned to the mission field. The next time they came home was two years later, after eight years. This time they shared with excitement that practically the whole of the village had been converted to Christ, and these new Christians were reaching out themselves, evangelising and winning those that were in neighbouring villages!

Praise God they didn't give up, but continued on faithfully in what God had called them to do. Now it isn't going to take us eight years before we see a breakthrough but the principle is clear. Before there could be any fruitfulness the couple had to first get a grasp of the language. They had to come alongside those they were trying to reach and had to win their respect. Much patience and commitment was needed as they sought to demonstrate practical Christianity with a consistent love for the people. It was then that the breakthrough came!

Thirdly, following on from what I've just said, we need to be able to identify ourselves with our friend. To be able to say, 'I know how you feel', without being patronising. Being real and honest with the person helps them to see that we do understand their struggles, and as we begin to open up about the things we've been through, it enables them in turn to do so even more. Paul could say to those he was reaching, *'we were ready to share with you not only the gospel of God but also our own selves'* (1 Thessalonians 2:8). This, I believe is crucial, to speak not just words, but to open our lives to them as well.

Obviously in doing this we've got to make sure that we're wise in what we share. We don't want to start a 'pity party' or to give the impression in any way that we can't cope with our own difficulties. Otherwise they will see that we have nothing much to offer them in their need and we'll end up with them counselling us! What we mean here, is to take the opportunity to identify with their needs when we've gone through similar things, but then to share how Christ has been such a strength and made all the difference.

One other thing on this point of identifying with people as they share their problems. We must be unshockable and never give any sense of disapproval as they talk about what they've been through. Also we need to be very aware of the importance to be loyal to them. If we are to strengthen the friendship they need to know that they can trust us and the things they share will be absolutely confidential.

Fourthly, be alert and quick to recognise their move towards you. As the relationship develops and you are starting to win their trust, they will in some way be trying to also reach out to you. It might be something very simple like the neighbour I referred to earlier. When I had cut her grass she came to me offering a bunch of flowers for my wife. She was in her own way trying to make some move towards me. Also the man who got his wife to ask me to move my car so the builders could put up scaffolding for his roof. In coming across the street smiling and chatting he was in his own way trying to make a move towards me. We need to be quick to recognise this and appreciate it when it happens.

Fifthly, as the friendship develops and opportunities arise to share our faith we must take care that we don't go over the top and undo the good work that has been developed. They must never feel pressurised by us, so we need to be sensitive in how much to share and how far to go. It's much better to be brief and to leave them wanting more, than to try to give them 'both barrels' of the gospel at once. Because of this some literature could be very useful. A bright leaflet, relevant book or interesting Christian paper could be helpful to have in mind. This is something they could read at their own pace, with no pressure and in the comfort of their own home. Perhaps even a short, thought-provoking video could also be considered. These things will then give us a future opportunity to pick up the conversation again by asking what they thought of the item that was given them.

Safeguards in the Friendship

This whole area of friendship evangelism could be like a minefield, full of potential danger. You often find that the thing God could use in the most fruitful way attracts particular attack from the enemy. It is for this reason that we must recognise some ground rules for our own protection. In James 4:4 we read, *'friendship with the world is enmity with God'* and in 2 Corinthians 6:17 *'come out from them, and be separate from them, says the Lord'*. Now this doesn't take away everything that has previously been said but it does show us that there is something to be on our guard against.

I believe what these scriptures are speaking of is the need for us to be 'distinctive disciples' and not 'chameleon Christians'. The chameleon is that amazing creature that is able to take on the same colourings as its background, becoming almost invisible as it merges in with its surroundings. If it walks across green grass and stops, it turns green. If it walks across a brick red wall and stops, it turns brick red. I wonder what would happen if it walked across a tartan colour – it would probably blow up!! We need to be distinctive and not those who merge into the surroundings that we are in, appearing no different from anyone else. There must be a distinctiveness about our values, attitudes, priorities and way of life.

Firstly, the basis on which we build must always be righteousness. The places that we go, that which we watch together, our conversation and the activities that we do, must remain pure. We will never win anyone by compromise. Only by a first class commitment to Christ can we ever expect to make any impression on our friend.

Secondly, our ultimate goal must always be to influence and win our friend for Christ. That doesn't mean we've always got to be speaking of Jesus, but it does mean that in our heart behind all that we do, this goal is always uppermost. The friendship should never be an end in itself for it is then that we start sliding into areas of compromise. I've had some people react quite strongly to the mention of this point, saying that this is wrong because it means that we have an ulterior motive behind what we're doing. I can't see any better or higher motive to have, than to love someone so much that you don't want to see them go to hell. The primary motive in the heart of Jesus in all that He did and said, was to *'seek and to save the lost'* (Luke 19:10).

Thirdly, be sure that your friendship is within your faith to see this person influenced in some positive way by your life and won into the Kingdom. It needs to be more than wishful thinking, *'without faith it is impossible to please God'* (Hebrews 11:6, NIV). One good way to help you see what you have faith for, is to ask yourself, 'can I imagine this person becoming a Christian?' If we can't even imagine it happening then it's a sure indication that we haven't got faith for it. If this is the case don't leave it there, aim to come to a place of faith for this person. The only way we can do that is as we turn to the Word of God and take hold of His promise for them. If you feed your faith your doubts will starve to death!

Fourthly, always choose your non-Christian friend from the same sex. That isn't to say that we shouldn't be friendly with the opposite sex, but this long term building needs to be righteous. The dangers are obvious. It is possible to start out with good sincere intentions, in a quite harmless friendship with an unconverted person of the opposite sex. In the end, however, our testimony and life can be ruined. The enthusiastic Christian young man that is trying to 'win' an attractive unconverted girl is wide open to deception and danger.

Some years ago at a Good News Crusade family camp in Malvern when I was part of the team, a middle-aged Christian man came to me for help. The night before he had brought a non-Christian woman friend to the meeting. She had got wonderfully saved that night and as he drove her back home, rejoicing in all that God had done, they stopped for a coffee at his house and ended up going to bed together!

Fifthly, have a goal in the early stages of the friendship somewhere along the line to make it clear that you are a Christian. We must nail our colours to the mast right at the beginning so that our friend is aware of our faith and commitment to Christ. This need not be any long testimony but just perhaps a simple comment in passing or short sentence. You'll find, especially if you've just changed jobs or perhaps moved house, maybe started at university, that the longer you leave making that stand the harder it will get to say anything.

Sixthly, one of the most practical safeguards is to share with another person, possibly your home group leader or one of the elders, the progress of the friendship. This will both encourage and strengthen you to know that someone else is supporting you. Also it will give you someone to go to that you can share your frustrations and disappointments with, and someone that you can look to for advice who has a more objective perspective of the situation.

Seventhly, the last safeguard and the most important is that of prayer. Everything that we do must be born out of and sustained in prayer. When we bring the friendship before God, it keeps us aware of our need of Him. We become more conscious of the righteous life that we need to have. Also, it is prayer that makes available to us amazing power that we do not have in ourselves. In James 5:16 (Amplified) we read that, *'The earnest, heartfelt, continued prayer of a righteous man makes tremendous power available, dynamic in its working.'* This speaks about an attitude of heart, a discipline of mind and a resolve of the will that refuses to give up on the person we're praying for.

As we pray we can be asking for God to bring an understanding to us of what might be the blockage in our friend's life. What is preventing them responding to Christ? As God shows us, we can take our authority in Jesus Name to bind the powers of darkness and loosen the hold that they have. We can be praying for them to receive a revelation from God that will bring a conviction of their own personal need. Unless God brings that revelation to open their blind eyes, they remain confused and oblivious to the urgency of their position. We could be praying about how our lifestyle can more clearly reveal Christ. What practical things we can do to strengthen the friendship and when is the right time to share our faith or invite them along to the meeting.

The principle of prayer is that whatever we ask in the will of the Father it shall be granted. So we can continuously bring our friend to God on the basis of His promise. God doesn't will the death of any sinner. It is God's will that they are saved through repentance and faith.

We find in God's word two reasons why He promises to give us a positive answer in the things we seek Him for. The first is that, *'the Father might be glorified in the Son'* (John 14:13) and the second is, *'that your joy might be full'* (John 16:24). Isn't it wonderful! When we've done all we can do in the friendship, God will do what we can't! He wants us to know the joy of seeing our friend come to Christ and through it all He will be glorified in their life.

8

The Baptism in the Holy Spirit

The founder of the Salvation Army, General Booth, could often be found pondering the pages of the book of Acts. As he did so invariably at some point or another, tears would start to flow down his face. With his head buried in his hands suddenly he would cry out in fervent prayer, 'Do it again Lord! Do it again!!' I'm sure that heartfelt desire can find an echo in the lives of many Christians today. There is a longing to see God's power touching the multitudes, and for our Christian witness to experience that same anointing as we find in the book of Acts. I've already made several references in passing concerning the importance of a Spirit-filled life and so I want us now to examine more closely this vital area.

It has well been said, 'If we major on God's word to the exclusion of the Holy Spirit we will dry up. If we emphasise the Holy Spirit and neglect the place of Scripture we will blow up, but when we hold both in high regard then we will grow up!' These two elements held in balance are essential not just for our maturity but also for an effective ministry. The power of the Holy Spirit must be the dynamic behind the mechanics of our evangelism, but what we embrace needs to be firmly grounded in God's word and not just experience.

D.L. Moody was an outstanding man of God who communicated the Gospel in a unique and effective way to his generation. He once said this about the Holy Spirit, 'I believe the gift of the Holy Ghost that is spoken of is a gift for certain but one that we have mislaid, overlooked and forgotten to seek for. If a man is only converted and we get him into church, we think the work is done, and we let him go right off to sleep instead of urging him to seek the gift of the Holy Ghost, that he may be anointed for the work. The world would soon be converted if all such were baptised with the Holy Ghost!' My heart says a loud AMEN to what this man of God felt so strongly. The anointing that comes from above is what we must seek if we are to win those around us.

What is the Baptism in the Holy Spirit?

There is inevitably a variety of opinions on this today. Some people feel it to be irrelevant as far as present day Church life is concerned. Others consider the experience was only for the Apostolic era. Something just for the New Testament Church to get it started and give it some 'impetus', (as though in some way we need that same power any the less today). Others maintain at conversion in that initial experience of new life, we received all that God had got for us.

I rather like what that great preacher Dr Martin Lloyd Jones had to say on this. His comment was, 'There is nothing that so quenches the Spirit as the teaching which identifies the Baptism of the Holy Ghost with regeneration. Some say you get it all when you are converted. If you got it all at conversion, in the name of God where is it?!' This is certainly a reasonable challenge and one that we must give consideration to.

I'm very aware that you cannot build truth on experience alone and so I deliberately want to be careful of being too subjective. Having said this, I believe we need to have the clear understanding that the baptism of the Holy Spirit is a definite experience. One that is subsequent to, and separate from, conversion. It is an encounter with God that equips us to live the life that Jesus lived in power, authority and victory.

The Holy Spirit brings us into God's kingdom but it is the anointing and fullness of God's Spirit that is necessary for effective service. As the Apostle Paul could say, *'For the kingdom of God does not consist in talk but in power'* (1 Corinthians 4:20). This anointing can break the yoke of every oppression and meet the needs of our generation today. There is no substitute for God's power.

Admittedly there can be found 'candy floss charismatics', who unfortunately in their over-enthusiasm have lacked wisdom and sensitivity. Candy floss is just 1½ ounces of sugar, some vanilla flavouring and some colouring. It is put into a spinner and whipped up until you have on the end of a stick an attractive display that looks very impressive. It appears quite eye-catching, as though you really have got something substantial. However, when you put it into your mouth – what a surprise! It disappears in seconds the moment your tongue touches it! Unfortunately this has been what others have observed in the lives of those who claimed to have experienced the fullness of the Holy Spirit. There has been a lot of outward show but underneath it all, very little substance.

No matter how true this might be in the case of some, it should never stop anyone seeking God for a new outpouring of His Spirit and greater measure of power upon their life. We can have confidence in seeking such an experience because of three main reasons.

Firstly, the Revelation of God's Word

We must begin to focus on what we discover in the Scriptures rather than upon other people's opinions or experiences. Throughout the Old Testament there are many occasions when God's anointing came upon people for a specific task transforming their lives. This can be seen in examples such as Balaam – (Numbers 24:2); Jephthah –

(Judges 11:29); Samson – (Judges 14:19); David – (1 Samuel 16:13); the messengers of Saul – (1 Samuel 19:20); Azariah the son of Oded – (2 Chronicles 15:1); Zechariah son of Jehoiada – (2 Chronicles 24:20) and Ezekiel – (Ezekiel 11:5).

These are only a few references, others could be mentioned, but one that is particularly clear speaks of God's promise to Saul. *'The spirit of the Lord will come mightily upon you, and you shall prophesy with them and be turned into another man.'* (1 Samuel 10:6.) In looking at such examples, we can see that the power of God was only given temporarily, to a relatively small number of people but the effect it had was dramatic. As we come into the New Testament though and indeed to present-day evangelism, we see that the outpouring of God's Power, is for all people everywhere who will believe.

In Joel 2:28, we have this prophetic word speaking of a future event.

> *'And it shall come to pass afterward, that I will pour out of my Spirit on all flesh; your sons and your daughters shall prophesy, your old men shall dream dreams, and your young men shall see visions. Even upon the menservants and maidservants in those days, I will pour out my Spirit.'*

Notice it was not intended to be in the lives of just a few, but rather upon all of God's people. It would be a supernatural outpouring of God's power, the effect of which would be to bring people into a new miraculous dimension of living.

Secondly, the Experience of the Disciples

Before Pentecost, prior to that mighty outpouring of God's Spirit which had been promised, Jesus breathed upon the disciples and said, *'Receive the Holy Spirit'* (John 20:22). At that moment these disciples received the Holy

Spirit and yet they were later to be baptised in the Holy Spirit on the Day of Pentecost.

Jesus gave careful instructions to His disciples saying:

> *'Behold, I send the promise of my Father upon you; but stay in the city, until you are clothed with power from on High.'* (Luke 24:49)

They were told not to begin their ministry until they had received this anointing. Also we read,

> *'while staying with them He charged them not to depart from Jerusalem, but to wait for the promise of the Father, which, He said, "you heard from me, for John baptized with water, but before many days you shall be baptized with the Holy Spirit."'* (Acts 1:4–5).

They had been with Jesus for three years, heard His teaching, seen His miracles and witnessed His death, burial and resurrection. You would think that they were well qualified to just get on and speak of Christ. However, the disciples were told to wait for that *'coming upon'* of power.

The Day of Pentecost arrives and while gathered together in the upper room the promise that they had been waiting for is actually fulfilled. *'. . . they were all filled with the Holy Spirit and began to speak in other tongues, as the Spirit gave them utterance'* (Acts 2:4). As a result, some were amazed and marvelled but others started to mock, saying, *'They're filled with new wine'* (v. 13). The same happens today when people are baptised in the Spirit. There are those who recognise that something wonderful is happening and others who react with criticism, or at best rationalise what they see. I can remember when I was baptised in the Holy Spirit. As I shared about it with others, some were glad and others were mad!

The next thing we see in the account of Pentecost is that

Peter stands up to explain what it was that was taking place. He says,

> *'For these men are not drunk, as you suppose, since it is only the third hour of the day; but this is what was spoken by the prophet Joel.'* (Acts 2:15 & 16)

He relates the promise of God's Word in Joel 2 with what they were experiencing at Pentecost. Peter then goes on to state that this experience was not just for them but,

> *'For the promise is to you, and to your children and to all that are far off, everyone whom the Lord our God calls to Him.'* (Acts 2:39)

The exciting thing is that, we are able, if we choose, to put our name in that verse and say, 'this promise is for me!'.

One important thing that we find in the experience of the disciples is that what happened to them was a 'gateway and not a goal'. Those who were baptised in Acts 2, were again filled in Acts 4, and continued to live in the power of God's Spirit. It was an on-going experience. We must never settle down in what we have received. If we do this we will start to lose our joy, liberty and power. It is vital when we have been baptised in the Spirit that we know we have not arrived. We are simply passing through a gateway into a whole new life in the Holy Spirit. The Bible says we are to, *'Be filled with the Spirit'* (Ephesians 5:18). In the Greek this is a continuous tense and really means, *'go on being filled'*.

Thirdly, the Example of Jesus

One of the most compelling arguments for our need to be baptised in the Holy Spirit is that which we find in the life of Christ. If it was necessary for Jesus to experience this, how much more do we need the same power and anointing to complete the tasks given to us. Jesus was conceived of the Holy Spirit. There was never a time when He was not fully God. The Holy Spirit was within Him yet we hear practically nothing of Jesus for thirty years, until a very special event took place.

Just prior to starting His public ministry He received God's anointing for the work He had to do. It was from this moment that a supernatural power was released upon His life. We read,

> 'Now when all the people were baptized, and when Jesus also had been baptized and was praying, the heaven was opened, and the Holy Spirit descended upon Him in bodily form, as a dove...'
>
> (Luke 3:21 & 22)

The Holy Spirit came upon Jesus and He was clothed with power from on high to fulfil His ministry effectively.

From that time on, never before, we read of Jesus that He was, *'full of the Holy Spirit'* (Luke 4:1). Also, *'Jesus returned in the power of the Spirit into Galilee, and a report concerning Him went out through all the surrounding country'* (v. 14). Then Jesus enters the temple and reads from the prophet Isaiah. He turns to the place where it was written, *'The Spirit of the Lord is upon me, ...'* (v. 18) and He concludes with his amazing statement, *'Today this scripture has been fulfilled in your hearing'* (v. 21).

Those in the temple looked at Him in surprise. Here He was in His home town where He had been raised and they said '... *Is this not Joseph's son?'* (v. 22). The Baptism of the Holy Spirit is able to change what appears to others as an ordinary life into something that is quite extraordinary – a life that brings glory to God and causes others to be amazed.

There can be no doubt that Jesus received the power of the Holy Spirit for service as the Bible says,

> '*God anointed Jesus of Nazareth with the Holy Spirit and with power...*' (Acts 10:38)

Even though Jesus was God in the flesh, the Scriptures are careful to record for our example and instruction that it was necessary for Him to know a supernatural anointing.
Jesus said,

> '*He who believes in me will also do the works that I do; and greater works than these will he do.*'
> (John 14:12)

I believe this is the heart's desire of God, with all due respect and reverence, that there might be little Jesuses moving around all across our land doing the same works that He did. 'An army of people' healing the sick, driving out demons and proclaiming the kingdom of God! How could we possibly do this without the same anointing of power? We need to dare to believe His word for those same works to be evident in our life and ministry.

Unmistakable Evidence of Having Received

Many years ago, after I'd received the fullness of the Spirit, someone came up to me after I'd finished preaching at my home Brethren church in Exeter. They said, 'You have been baptised in the Spirit, haven't you? I can see the difference on your face!' Any true encounter with the Lord leaves its mark upon our life in a way that others cannot help but notice, just as was the case with Moses. When he came down from Mount Sinai having met with God, his face shone with the glory of the Lord (Exodus 34:29). The disciples because of their boldness, caused those around to recognise that they had been with Jesus (Acts 4:13).

I believe the evidence is clear if we have received the fullness of the Spirit. As we look at this let us consider four things that ought to be noticeable in our lives.

Firstly, the initial evidence that we find in the Scriptures is the gift of tongues. The first thing that happened to the disciples was, *'they were all filled with the Holy Spirit and began to speak in other tongues as the Spirit gave them utterance'* (Acts 2:4). In this particular case at Pentecost it was a definite clear language that they had never learnt themselves, but was known by those listening.

When I was baptised in the Holy Spirit, nothing dramatic happened, not even any great feelings were experienced, but as I was prayed for, I began to speak in another tongue. Just a few syllables at first, then this was followed by a greater flow. It is so important to have that evidence because until this comes, there is always that seed of doubt about whether we have really received. Throughout the book of Acts we find this evidence was not the exception but rather the rule.

The gift of tongues is something that every person can experience when they are baptised in the Holy Spirit. Not everyone does, but I believe every person can. Jesus taught that tongues were a sign of our believing in His word (Mark 16:17). The Apostle Paul went on to explain why tongues were so important. He teaches, *'one who speaks in a tongue speaks not to men but to God'* (1 Corinthians 14:2). It is a prayer language expressing ourself to the Lord.

Paul also says in the same chapter, *'He who speaks in a tongue edifies himself'* (v. 4). We all get occasions when through disappointment and discouragement we need strengthening, and this is an added benefit of the gift – we grow stronger. I don't know how it works, but God's Word says it does and that's good enough for me. Paul goes on to teach that tongues with an interpretation brings a message to the church. '... *He who prophesies is greater than he who speaks in tongues, unless someone interprets, so that the church may be edified'* (v. 5). This application of the gift catches everyone's attention. As the tongue is given people become more alert and realise that God is about to speak.

Secondly, another sign which is unmistakable is that of dynamic Power. *'You shall receive power when the Holy Spirit has come upon you; and you shall be my witnesses'* (Acts 1:8). It is not merely spiritual gifts, clapping and celebration that is of primary importance, but supernatural power – an ability outside ourselves that comes from God. In the book of Acts we read that, *'With great power the Apostles gave their testimony to the resurrection of the Lord Jesus'* (Acts 4:33). This was one of the most obvious and necessary characteristics of their evangelism. The miracles of healing and deliverance were an expression of God at work through them in power. The result of this is that it gives 'spiritual muscle' to our authority as disciples of Christ.

When I received the baptism of the Holy Spirit, there came to me a new confidence and security in God. This anointing is able to rid our lives of all inferiority and feelings of inadequacy giving us a new Holy Boldness. In Acts 2 we find that as the anointing of God's Spirit came upon Peter, he was a new man. He preached with fearlessness and about three thousand people were converted. Then in Acts 4, his sermon resulted in five thousand being saved. The disciples who were behind locked doors for fear of the Jews were transformed by God's power, and part of the people who turned the world upside down!

Thirdly, a new enthusiasm and liberty grips our heart and Jesus becomes more real to us as a person, not just as a doctrine. The apostle Paul's prayer which became an all consuming passion in his life was, *'That I might know Him and the power of His resurrection'* (Philippians 3:10). A new love for Jesus, and also for the basic principles of Christian living becomes evident. We read of the first disciples that, *'They devoted themselves to the Apostles' teaching and fellowship, to the breaking of bread and the prayers'* (Acts 2:42). These areas that are vital to our relationship with Christ can become more of a duty than a delight, but the outpouring of God's Spirit upon us brings a new devotion to them.

Even when faced with hardship and difficult times, there is a supernatural joy in the Holy Spirit that becomes our strength. Our enthusiasm is not dampened by the problems of life. Rather the ability to overcome and walk consistently in victory is made a greater reality. The Christians in Acts were quite amazing in this respect. Having been arrested, beaten and threatened we read that,

> 'They left the presence of the council, rejoicing that they were counted worthy to suffer dishonour for the Name. And every day in the temple and at home they did not cease teaching and preaching Jesus as the Christ.' (Acts 5:41–42)

Fourthly, the evidence of a Christlike character, comes through being filled with God's Spirit. The gift of tongues, supernatural power and great enthusiasm is wonderful but there must be more than this. There needs to be a Christlikeness in the quality of our character. The fruit of a spirit-filled life is, '*love, joy, peace, patience, kindness, goodness, faithfulness, gentleness, self-control*' (Galatians 5:22). What a beautiful picture of Jesus we find here. This is what the world needs to see, the character of Christ lifted up in our life.

Notice also we are talking about the 'Holy' Spirit. The pure and righteous character of Christ in a genuine Spirit-filled life is something that will become evident to all. Our attitudes, thoughts, words, motives and actions cannot help but be purified by the fire of God's Holy Spirit.

Things that Can Hinder Our Receiving

Firstly, what will always be a problem to us, in receiving the baptism of the Holy Spirit and indeed any of God's gifts, is unconfessed sin. Unrighteousness grieves the Holy Spirit and hinders the release of God's power into a person's life. The Bible says:

> *'If our hearts do not condemn us, we have confidence before God; and we receive from Him whatever we ask.'*
> (1 John 3:21)

This verse is equally true the other way round. If our heart does condemn us we have no confidence before God, and will not receive the things for which we ask. Sin needs to be dealt with and confessed before we come to receive from God, especially any past involvement with the occult. I have come across many situations in counselling when people have not come through in tongues nor have the assurance of what they'd asked for, because of past involvement in the occult.

Secondly, doubt is something that affects us receiving. If we are in two minds about what we are seeking for, or perhaps we're not quite sure and not fully convinced, then this uncertainty will rob us of what God wants to give. A double-minded man will not only be unstable in all his ways, and not just be tossed around like the waves of the sea but, *'he will not receive anything from the Lord'* (James 1:8). Single-minded faith is what God looks for. The baptism of the Holy Spirit can only be experienced by faith, as we take God at His word. The Bible says,

> *'Whoever would draw near to God must believe that He exists and that He rewards those who seek Him.'*
> (Hebrews 11:6)

We need not get all worked up and complicated, but simply come as a child to its father with confidence that what He has promised He wants to give. There is certainly no reluctance in the heart of God. He wants to give more than we want to receive, because He knows it is important for our development. We have not got to wrestle with God to persuade Him. We come as a child, fix attention on the Giver, and ask with an expectancy to receive.

The Bible says,

> 'Ask, and it will be given you; seek, and you will find; knock, and it will be opened to you. For everyone who asks receives, and he who seeks finds, and to him who knocks it will be opened ... if you then, who are evil, know how to give good gifts to your children, how much more will the heavenly father give the Holy Spirit to those who ask him!' (Luke 11:9–13)

Thirdly, another thing that stops us receiving is very simple and straightforward. Sometimes we just don't ask. The Bible says, *'You do not have, because you do not ask'* (James 4:2). At times this is because of pride, maybe tradition, perhaps fear, or just through apathy. People don't even bother to ask God. They then wonder why their life is not showing the power and liberty that they see in others.

Someone who was a great help to me in my life, but certainly wasn't at that time very keen on any talk of spiritual gifts, used to say, 'Brother, I believe in the gifts and in the anointing of God's Spirit and if He wants me to have them, He will give them to me, in His time.' One day I said to him, 'Brother, did you have that sort of approach to receiving God's gift of forgiveness and eternal life when you were saved? Or did you recognise your need, realise God's promise, and reach out to the Lord whole-heartedly to receive?' As I said this, it dawned on him that if he'd waited without asking, saying, 'in your time,' he never would have found salvation. The same is true of all that God wants to give that is promised in His Word. If we don't ask we don't receive!

Fourthly – Yet another reason for our failing to receive is asking for the wrong reasons. Having a wrong motive can be a blockage. James tells us, *'you ask and do not receive, because you ask wrongly, to spend it on your passions'* (James 4:3). Maybe the reason why we want the baptism in the Spirit or gift of tongues is to be like everyone else. Perhaps just to have a 'nice' experience, or maybe to be noticed as someone who is spiritual. Our motive must be that of Acts 1:8 *'to be a witness'*. Our desire needs to be, 'Lord I want to be more effective in service for you. I want to bring glory to your name.' It is not to glorify the gifts, the experience or even ourselves, but to bring honour to the Lord.

9

The Good News of God's
Healing Power

An old story is told about a country boy who went to visit
his friend in the big city. As they walked down the main
High Street of the busy town, suddenly the country boy
stopped and said, 'I can hear a cricket!' The city boy
laughed and said, 'you couldn't possibly hear anything like
that. We've got the noise of the construction work behind
us, the roar of traffic in front of us and the bustle of
shopping all around us. It would be impossible to hear a
cricket!' But sure enough, he reached into the crevice of a
building nearby and pulled out a short black cricket. The
city boy said, 'that's amazing. However did you do it?'
Smiling, the country boy dipped into his pocket and said
'you watch.' He then took out a handful of coins and threw
them up into the air. As they came tinkling down onto the
pavement, suddenly everyone spun round and froze! 'Do
you see,' said the country boy. 'It depends what you're
listening for!!'

There are so many voices all around us today, of doubt,
prejudice, tradition and rational thinking. We can find
ourselves hearing only them and not listening to what God
is saying. For our evangelism to attract the interest and
hold the attention of others, people need to see the miraculous healing power of God. It is this that causes them to
sit up and take notice of what we are wanting to share. The

effect of miracles in the days of Jesus certainly made a significant impact then, and still does today.

The result of when a man came to Jesus *'full of leprosy'* and was healed, caused many people to be drawn to Christ. Luke tells us,

> *'So much more the report went abroad concerning Him; and great multitudes gathered to hear and be healed of their infirmities.'* (Luke 5:15)

Miracles of healing create a faith environment to preach the gospel. Multitudes couldn't get to the 'meeting' quick enough! When healing takes place our preaching makes sense to people and they respond. Even the religious were stirred and travelled many miles looking for Jesus because of His miraculous power. Verse 17 says,

> *'On one of those days, as He was teaching, there were Pharisees and teachers of the law sitting by, who had come from every village of Galilee and Judea and from Jerusalem.'*

In the book of Acts we find that because of the healing of a man who had been lame forty years from birth, it gave a unique opportunity to preach the gospel. Although there was opposition, people were also open to respond. *'Many of those who heard the word believed; and the number of the men came to about five thousand'* (Acts 4:4). Later on Aene'as who'd been paralysed for eight years was wonderfully healed with the result that, *'all the residents of Lydda and Sharon saw him, and they turned to the Lord'* (Acts 9:35). Then in the same chapter Peter is asked to come to a place called Joppa because a disciple by the name of Tabitha had just died. He miraculously raised her from the dead, and this had the effect that *'It became known throughout all Joppa, and many believed in the Lord'* (v. 42). The evidence of miracles convinces people of the truth of the Gospel and brings the reality of God's presence in such a way that is hard to ignore or dispute.

As three Christians discussed together the subject of miracles the first asked, 'What are miracles?' 'Well,' replied the second confidently, 'a miracle happens when God does exactly what our minister asks.' 'Really,' said the third. 'We think it's a miracle when our minister does exactly what God asks!' While this might sound amusing I'm sure we can all think of those who are frustrated with this sort of situation. Miracles do still happen today, but for these to become more evident in our evangelism we've got to be obedient to what God says. We must listen to God's word and not the muddled thinking or fears of other people.

Smith Wigglesworth was a man used in an outstanding way to bring healing to thousands. One of his famous sayings was, 'we miss the grandeur because we lack the audacity!' How true this is. God wants to move mightily through our lives, bringing healing to others, but we've got to have the audacity to act upon what He says. The Bible tells us, *'Jesus Christ is the same yesterday and today and forever'* (Hebrews 13:8). Believing this ought to give us all the confidence and boldness we should ever need. It is true that doctors, hospitals and medicine all play an important role in God's purpose to restore people back to health. However this should never distract us from having confidence in the miraculous healing power of Jesus.

With God All Things Are Possible

About seventeen years ago, before I became a Christian, I used to visit a whole range of denominations in my search for God. I recall attending a Pentecostal church in Exeter, sitting on the back row and being fascinated by all that was taking place. As these people sang a chorus, they didn't do so once or twice, but dozens of times! When they prayed, they all prayed together, at the tops of their voices. Then when the preacher stood up to give his sermon, they were not quiet and passive. They started to shout out, 'Amen!' 'Preach it brother!' 'Hallelujah!' Those people really seemed to believe something that I'd not found in other churches.

One particular chorus which was sung that night, made a deep impression upon me. The words were,

> 'Have you got any rivers you think are uncrossable?
> Have you got any mountains you can't tunnel through?
> God specialises in things thought impossible.
> He can do just what none other can do!'

This statement of God's miraculous power not only changed my life then, it has given me the most exciting and wonderful message to preach in my ministry as an evangelist today. Central to the gospel is the amazing truth, the good news that, *'What is impossible with men is possible with God'* (Luke 18:27).

While speaking at a church at Welling, near Malvern, I was staying with the pastor and his wife. As we were sitting in the living room talking, he called in his daughter to where we were. This beautiful seven year old girl, with lovely long brown hair, came bounding up and he introduced her to me. They said, 'you prayed for our daughter four years ago when she was seriously ill with a condition called, "Polycystic kidneys". The doctors had told us that she'd got just three months before her kidneys would completely fail. At that time the colour of her skin was yellowish and she had lost most of her hair. You prayed for her those years ago and here she is today, completely healed and restored!' They said, 'the very day after prayer she changed from looking the colour she was to a beautiful pink, and God has wonderfully healed her!'

On another occasion during a Celebration Meeting that I was taking down in London, a vicar and his wife came forward for prayer. The couple desperately wanted a baby but the doctors had told them that it wasn't possible. This was because the husband had suffered with cancer in that region of his body that had left him sterile. They responded in faith believing in the healing power of God. I prayed for them and asked the Lord to do what only He could do in this situation. Just under four months later I was speaking with his wife on the phone. She said to me, 'Yan, I've got good news for you. I'm over three and a half months pregnant and it's left a lot of doctors with open mouths!'

We live in a world that is full of sceptics. Our secular society is constantly doubting not only what God is able to do but also whether God even exists. As we consider God's healing power today, it's crucial even as Christians that we don't allow our intellectual doubts, or our personal fears to rob us of the full gospel that we have been called to proclaim.

'What is the Gospel?'

This might sound like a very straightforward and obvious question at first. However, I believe it's because we fail to recognise the 'full gospel' that we see only limited results. It is helpful to re-examine the 'good news' that has been entrusted to us.

The Bible presents the Gospel's good news as far more than John 3:16, glorious and thrilling though this is. It is broader than just receiving forgiveness for our sins and being saved from a lost eternity. The full gospel is the Good News that through faith in Christ and His finished work on the cross we can be made whole – spiritually, emotionally and physically. Throughout Scripture we see that God saves, heals, forgives, restores and delivers those who will put their trust in Him.

The gospel is, *'the testimony of God'* (1 Corinthians 2:1). That is, His word to us. Not the logic of man but the word of Almighty God. The gospel is also, *'the power of God'* (Romans 1:16). His ability to fulfil His Word. In the gospel we find that the message and the miraculous go together, one without the other is incomplete. The two are vital. The message communicates truth and the miraculous convinces us of its reality.

To see clearly what the gospel is, we only need to look at the mission of Jesus, in both His words and His deeds. As far as His words were concerned, He brought a message of hope into a sin-sick, broken world. Jesus said,

> *'The Spirit of the Lord is upon me, because He has anointed me to preach Good News to the poor. He has sent me to proclaim release to the captives, and recovering of sight to the blind, to set at liberty those who are oppressed...'* (Luke 4:18)

Then through the deeds of Jesus we see miraculous healing coming to confirm what He was speaking. Throughout His ministry, cripples walked, lepers were cleansed, the deaf heard and the blind received their sight.

Jesus through His deeds revealed the heart of God towards us. Everything He did was to make known God's will. Jesus said,

> *'the Son can do nothing of His own accord, but only what He sees the Father doing; for whatever He does, that the Son does likewise.'* (John 5:19)

The message Jesus preached and the miracles that took place show us how God feels about sickness.

As far as Jesus was concerned, healing sickness and delivering people from oppression was an integral part of the gospel. This went hand in hand with preaching the Word. Where Christ was signs and wonders were the norm. He didn't have to advertise prayer for the sick or have great healing crusades, yet everywhere Jesus went miracles took place.

Later on Jesus says to His disciples, '... *As the Father has sent me, even so I send you*' (John 20:21). It was one thing for Jesus to work the miracles, but now He is saying, 'just as I've been sent by my Father, I want to send you'! An unmistakable commission was given to the disciples for them to declare and demonstrate the same message.

The gospel is seen in what the disciples were instructed to do. We read,

> '*He called to Him His twelve disciples and gave them authority over unclean spirits, to cast them out, and to heal every disease and every infirmity.*'
>
> (Matthew 10:1)

Then next we see He sent out the seventy to, '*heal the sick in it, and say to them, "the Kingdom of God has come near to you"*' (Luke 10:9).

This commission that was given to the twelve and also to the seventy was then extended to every believer. Some of the last words that Jesus spoke before He ascended back to heaven show what was to be the normal pattern for evangelism – to preach the word and bring healing to mankind in the authority of His name. Jesus said,

> '*And these signs shall accompany those who believe: in my Name ... they will lay their hands on the sick, and they will recover.*'   (Mark 16:17–18)

The obedience of the disciples to this commission is seen throughout the book of Acts with the same consistency of the message and the miraculous working together.

In the Epistles Paul tells us how he made clear the gospel. He said,

> '*I will not venture to speak of anything except what Christ has wrought through me to win obedience from the Gentiles, by word and deed, by the power of signs and wonders...*'   (Romans 15:18 & 19)

119

The Word is important. We need to believe the Word, preach the Word, and stand on the Word – that's vital. The deed is also essential. Our practical expression of love helps people to see the genuine concern we have for their needs. This third aspect though, is often the missing element in the gospel presentation of today, 'the power of signs and wonders in the Holy Spirit.'

Moving on in the Bible, as we come to the book of James, explicit instructions show what the normal practice of the Church should be to meet the needs of the sick. We read,

> *'Let him call for the elders of the Church, and let them pray over him, anointing him with oil in the Name of the Lord; and the prayer of faith will save the sick man and the Lord will raise him up.'*   (James 5:14–15)

Praise God that His word is so emphatic and definite, *'the prayer of faith **will** save the sick and the Lord **will** raise him up.'*

Just as God never left us without a ransom for sin, so too, He has not left us without a remedy for sickness. That's good news – what a gospel! This is what we have to preach to mankind and to meet the needs that are all around us today. Through miraculous power God is revealed to people, not in abstract terms, or in a way that is impersonal but in ways that are real and meaningful. When healing comes to an individual and they are released from their affliction, then they know there is a God that cares.

During a time of ministry at a church in Somerset, one of the leaders came forward for prayer. This man had a severe, painful, back condition for over ten years. Often it would be so bad that he'd need to be off work for two weeks and just stay at home in agony. There didn't seem to be a lot that could be done for him. On the occasion I was at the church it was actually during one of these periods that he was off work in much pain. As I prayed in the Name of Jesus the healing touch of God came down upon him and he was instantly released there and then. Turning to the congregation he gave testimony that the pain he came with that night had completely gone!

That evening he went to bed and when he got up the following morning, there was still no pain. He then went out to his next door neighbour and shared about the way God had healed him. Also while speaking to one of his unconverted relatives on the phone he told them his testimony of healing. That miracle has been a message to his neighbour and relative of the reality of the gospel that can't be disputed!

'Who Can Experience Its Power?'

Paul says,

> 'The gospel is the power of God to everyone who believes.' (Romans 1:16)

Faith is the key. It is an essential part of the healing process. We need to believe in what God is able to do. The woman in the Bible who had a haemorrhage condition had been sick for twelve years. Having been healed she heard these words from Jesus, 'your faith has made you well' (Luke 8:48). Again in the case of Bartimae'us, he cried out for a miracle, wanting Jesus to heal his blind eyes. His sight was restored and then Jesus said, 'go your way, your faith has made you well' (Mark 10:52).

A step of faith is important, not based on our feelings or understanding, but on the authority of God's word. Faith expressed in action is vital. The Bible says, 'according to your faith be it done to you' (Matthew 9:29). By the measure of our faith we begin to experience the fulfilment of God's word.

While preaching at a meeting in Barnstaple, one lady came forward with her fingers crippled and bent with arthritis. She also had metal callipers on both wrists because of a brittle bone condition and her hands were bandaged up. Doctors had told her she would need to wear the metal supports for the rest of her life. As I prayed for her, there was an immediate response of faith. She ripped off her bandages and callipers and was able to move her fingers and wrists freely. She was wonderfully healed that night and I've been back to the church at least three times since and she is still healed today!

In Mark 9:23 we read, *'All things are possible to him who believes'*. These were the words of Jesus spoken to the father of a boy who had a deaf and dumb spirit. As he came asking for Jesus to help his son, he realised the lack of faith in his life. The response of the father to the words of encouragement that Jesus spoke were, *'I do believe; help me overcome my unbelief!'* (Mark 9:24, NIV).

We see in this, that even when we have faith for some things, there can be other areas of our life where there is unbelief and doubts. Faith and unbelief can be in our life at the same time! We might have faith for evangelism, perhaps faith in the ministry of music or maybe faith for our Sunday School class to be brought to salvation. But then when it comes to areas of healing or deliverance we can find ourselves having doubts and areas of unbelief. Unbelief restricts the power of God today just as it did two thousand years ago in the village of Nazareth. The Bible says of Jesus, *'He did not do many mighty works there, because of their unbelief'* (Matthew 13:58).

The Will of God in Healing

To help people come to a place of faith we need to know the will of God in healing. Knowing in our heart that it is God's will to heal is very important. Some people say, 'how do I know it's God's will to heal me?' Well, the will of God is found in the Word of God. The Bible is God's last will and testament, God's final word on the issue. When we are sick, to delay coming for prayer with the thought, 'Is it God's will to heal me?' is like standing at a bus stop waiting for a bus that is already there! Let us then take a closer look at what the Word of God says.

Firstly, looking in the Old Tetament for examples that relate to physical sickness we have this statement, *'I am the Lord that healeth thee'* (Exodus 15:26, AV). We also read in the Psalms of God, *'Who forgives all your iniquity, who heals all your diseases'* (Psalm 103:3). Then in Isaiah 53:5, *'Upon Him was the chastisement that made us whole, and with His stripes we are healed.'* This should encourage us, for we find a firm basis in the Old Testament to build our faith.

Secondly, as we come to the New Testament we see just as clearly the will of God concerning healing:

> *'Wherever He went – into villages, towns or countryside – they placed the sick in the market places. They begged Him to let them touch even the edge of His cloak, and all who touched Him were healed.'*
>
> (Mark 6:56, NIV)

Also we find,

> *'That evening they brought to Him many who were possessed with demons, and He cast out the spirits with a word, and healed all who were sick.'*
>
> (Matthew 8:16)

Then again we find,

> *'Jesus went about all the cities and villages, teaching in their synagogues and preaching the gospel of the Kingdom, and healing every disease and every infirmity.'*
>
> (Matthew 9:35)

Healing Comes in Different Ways

We can't predict or dictate how, or even when, healing should happen. There is no formula that we can tie God to. The way healing comes is often varied. For example, sometimes the healing will be instant. We don't have any problem with that miracle. Most of the healings that took place in the Bible were like this. The man I prayed for from Somerset with that back condition and the woman from Barnstaple with her arthritis and brittle bones were instantly healed. When healing is instant it is always wonderful and exciting, but this doesn't always happen.

On occasions healing will be gradual and need further prayer. For example in Mark 8:23 we find a blind man coming to Jesus, and the Lord ministers to him. The man's eyes aren't immediately restored. He doesn't instantly see clearly. The man says, *'I see men, but they look like trees walking'* (v. 24). There was blurred vision, he couldn't see completely. Jesus laid hands upon him again and ministered further, then his sight was restored. From experience this can be the case. Something will start as a person comes forward for prayer, and yet the healing will be gradual and need further prayer.

In other instances the healing will be linked to obedience. We find this in the case of Naaman the leper. He was told that he had to go and wash in the river seven times. He was a bit reluctant to do this at first, but as he obeyed those instructions the Bible says, *'his flesh was restored like the flesh of a little child, and he was clean'* (2 Kings 5:14). The skin of that man was miraculously restored to its original condition. This point of obedience is again seen in the account of the ten lepers that came to the Lord for healing. Jesus told them, *'go and show yourselves to the priest'* (Luke 17:14). We then read in the same verse, *'as they went they were cleansed!'* They weren't healed immediately, but it was as they obeyed, that healing came.

Sometimes the miracle people are looking to God for, is delayed. This is puzzling and often causes great difficulty.

When God doesn't appear to answer prayer and doesn't seem to be doing anything, it's then that people struggle with what is happening. However, if we can see from the Scriptures that this can be the case then we can still believe for the Lord to do something. God's delays are not necessarily His denials.

We see an example of a miracle that was delayed in the case of Lazarus. People came to Jesus telling Him about the serious condition of His friend. In hearing about his state the scripture says,

> 'Now Jesus loved Martha and her sister and Lazarus. So when He heard that he was ill, He stayed two days longer in the place where He was.'   (John 11:5–6)

Jesus deliberately delayed and as a result Lazarus died. Even though Jesus didn't immediately respond, He did arrive and performed a tremendous miracle as He raised Lazarus from the dead!

What About Those Who Are Not Healed?

I believe we need to be real and honest with those that we pray for. Sometimes people are not healed and we just haven't got an answer as to why. We should never try and convince people that they have 'received their healing', when clearly they haven't. Some of the extreme faith teaching today that would try to persuade people to think like this is very harmful, and I certainly question the integrity of such ministers. Careful and sensitive counselling with those who have not been healed is helpful. Without loading any guilt onto an already discouraged life, we need to consider if there is anything that might be hindering their healing.

Many reasons could be offered as to why some are not healed. For example, unbelief, unconfessed sin, or the sickness being rooted in anxiety and stress. Perhaps an attitude of bitterness and resentment has brought on the illness and needs to be repented of. With some people they might subconsciously not want to be healed because they're holding on to their condition for attention and sympathy or an escape from responsibility, perhaps even as an excuse for other areas of life that they feel inadequate in. Their reasoning can be that if they are sick, then other people will be more understanding and not expect too much from them.

Another reason for why some might not be healed could quite simply be that it isn't yet the Lord's time for them. This is a point that can be helpful and one we read of in Luke 5:15–16:

> 'and great multitudes gathered to hear and be healed of their infirmities. But He withdrew to the wilderness and prayed.'

The needs of the people were many. They had come with faith and expectancy for Jesus to heal them but this wasn't to be their moment.

So there are many reasons that we could give and things that we've got to examine carefully to help people come to a place of faith. At the end of the day though, we've got to acknowledge that we only know in part, as though we're looking through a darkened glass. When we've done our best and sought to be obedient in presenting Christ as the healer, we must simply leave the matter with God and acknowledge that He alone knows.

10

Declaring the Deliverance of God

One of the most dramatic questions that was ever asked in
the Bible was expressed by a King called Darius. He found
himself manipulated into the position of having to send
Daniel to the lions. He didn't want to do it, but in his
weakness he allowed Daniel to be taken away. That night
he was so restless that he rose up early before day to see
the consequences of his decision. As he anxiously
approached the lions' den he cried out in a tone of
anguish,

> 'O Daniel, servant of the living God, has your God,
> whom you serve continually, been able to deliver you
> from the lions?'   (Daniel 6:20)

What a tremendous position for Daniel to be in, to be able
to stand up and in effect declare – 'Hallelujah – yes He
has!'

We need this confidence in God's ability to deliver,
especially in the area of any demonic power that is afflic-
ting those we are aiming to win for Christ. Deliverance
from the influence of evil spirits is as necessary today as it
was two thousand years ago. In outreach we will certainly
come up against the need to bring release into the lives of
others.

Any book on equipping God's people for the work of

evangelism would be incomplete without such an important subject being addressed. However, as we take a look at deliverance we must be careful of the extremes that can be seen in the Christian ministry today. Excesses where, in some cases, the devil is blamed for everything, and people see a demon under every 'cornflake'! Then on the other hand, there are those who refuse to acknowledge the satanic dimension of people's problems. One of the great strategies of the enemy is to cause the Church to swing from one extreme to the other. In doing so, we fail to come to a firm foundation of truth that has the power to set people free.

The responsibility of every Christian is to be able to declare the deliverance of God from a personal conviction of its truth. Before launching into the ministry of deliverance, we need to know the reality of it in our own lives. This enables us to minister from a place of confidence in the power of God, and not simply from theory.

The Influence of Demons

The aims of Satan with his host of demons, are to *spoil* a person's relationship with God, to *steal* from them God's best, and ultimately to *separate* people from God's presence. We can find throughout the Scriptures the activity of evil spirits. Their strategy is very clear and it has to be said, very effective. These demon powers come to:

Oppress – that is to bring a sense of heaviness, depression, or restriction, to a person's life. The Bible says,

> *'God anointed Jesus of Nazareth with the Holy Spirit and with power; how he went about doing good and healing all that were oppressed by the devil.'*
>
> (Acts 10:38)

One elderly lady from Barnstaple that I prayed with over a year ago, asked for help because for ten years she had been oppressed with migraine headaches. At times they'd get so bad that she would have to spend several days in bed. As the spirit of oppression was bound, she was completely set free that night. I've been back to the church several times since then, and she has not been troubled any further with these headaches.

Deceive – Satan has been a deceiver from the beginning of creation. The spirit of deception is at work now, probably more so than at any other time. We read about the end times that,

> *'some will abandon the faith and follow deceiving spirits and things taught by demons.'*
>
> (1 Timothy 4:1, NIV)

So many people, even in the Church, have been led astray, and have gone out of God's will into error. They open themselves up to a spirit of deception, and continue on a path that is contrary to God's word.

I can remember being at an Anglican church not long ago speaking about the danger of deception. After the meeting a man came up to me and said, 'The Lord has told me I have got to divorce my wife!' ... When I asked why, he said, 'my wife plays Bingo and I can't stand Bingo!' He said, 'God is calling me to Romania and Russia to share the Gospel, so I've got to divorce my wife!' Nothing I said would convince him that he was being deceived, in fact he went on to say, 'Many leaders have told me that I'm wrong, but God has said I'm right!' Not only is that man deceived by the enemy and heading towards disaster, he is going to cause disaster wherever he goes.

Torment – The apostle Paul came to Timothy with this message,

> *'For God hath not given us the spirit of fear...'*
>
> (2 Timothy 1:7, AV)

When people are tormented by insecurities and deep-rooted feelings of inferiority, it has the effect of restricting their life. They are robbed of their peace and we can be sure that the enemy is at work. This is especially so in the area of irrational fears and phobias.

A team member and myself prayed for a lady from a Pentecostal church in Somerset. This person had been bound by phobias for nearly forty years. She had a phobia of the dark, of enclosed spaces, and of water. The most gripping and tormenting phobia in her life though, was a fear of 'vomiting'. Although she knew it was irrational, her life for all those years had been tormented by these fears. Just to sit down calmly in a counselling situation, and to even mention the word 'vomiting' brought an immediate reaction. Literally, without any exaggeration, she was thrown from the state of being calm to a state of hysteria in a matter of seconds. I praise God that before the end of that weekend we were able to minister deliverance to her, and she was completely released from the torment of her fears.

Drive and Compel – In the gospels we read of a man in the grip of demonic powers,

> '*He was kept under guard, and bound with chains and fetters, but he broke the bonds and was driven by the demon into the desert.*'   (Luke 8:29)

Almost anything which has a compulsive effect upon people, and becomes obsessive to the point where they feel driven to act in a certain way, can have a demonic root. It may be an eating disorder, or it could be certain habits like alcohol or drug abuse, perhaps gambling, gluttony, smoking, lust, homosexuality, and perversions. In some cases an obsession about fitness or our figure can be an area of spiritual bondage. What might start off as something harmless, but develops into a compulsion, is almost certainly demonic.

130

One man that I ministered to in Chorley was bound by a compulsive spirit. He said that he'd broken all the ten commandments except one, in as many days. He'd also tried to commit suicide on the motorway by driving his car into the back of a lorry. As he came forward for prayer that night he repented of all areas of sin and asked Jesus to be Lord of his life. We began to pray about the evil powers that had been driving him and immediately demons started to manifest. Anger, bitterness and violence started to erupt. As we prayed over him it took four people to hold him down. After deliverance took place he looked a changed man, and completely peaceful.

The Scriptural Basis for Deliverance

Again, as with everything that I've said in this book we must come back to Scripture for a firm foundation. To accept and move in the deliverance ministry we need to look to God's Word for our understanding. As we do so we'll see that Scripture is very clear.

Firstly, throughout Christ's ministry He not only healed the sick, but He cast out demons. Jesus brought release to the captives,

> 'That evening they brought to Him many who were possessed with demons, and He cast out the spirits with a word.' (Matthew 8:16)

There was tremendous authority in the ministry of Jesus over evil powers. All it took was one word and demons had to go. We read also,

> 'As they were going away, behold a dumb demoniac was brought to Him. And when the demon had been cast out, the dumb man spoke.' (Matthew 9:32–33)

On one occasion the orderly gathering of worshippers was interrupted by someone among them who had an evil spirit. However, Jesus soon dealt with the situation; we read,

> 'Jesus rebuked him, saying, "Be silent, and come out of him!", and when the demon had thrown him down in the midst, he came out of him, having done him no harm.'
> (Luke 4:35)

Secondly, the commission Jesus gave to His disciples in Mark 16:17 was to, 'cast out demons'. Notice He did not say, 'Coax them out' or 'Counsel them to come out'. Jesus said drive them out! When we go forward for Christ in the authority of His name, every demonic power must go! Jesus won that glorious victory on the cross. It was there that He triumphed over every evil power. Through the message of the Gospel we are instructed to drive out every demonic presence that is restricting the lives of people from living for Christ.

Thirdly, there is the practice of the New Testament church as they continued in obedience to that original commission. We see this was very much the case in the ministry of Philip as he proclaimed Christ in Samaria. The Bible says,

> 'Multitudes with one accord gave heed to what was being said by Philip, when they heard him and saw the signs which he did. For unclean spirits came out of many who were possessed, crying with a loud voice.'
> (Acts 8:6–7)

Also in the preaching of Paul we read,

> 'God did extraordinary miracles by the hand of Paul, so that handkerchiefs or aprons were carried away

132

> *from his body to the sick, and diseases left them and
> the evil spirits came out of them.'*   (Acts 19:11–12)

This ability to deliver should be more evident in the ministry of Christians today. It certainly gives each of us a challenge, but also a goal to pray towards.

Sadly, deliverance is an area that many churches would rather steer away from, often because of fear of the consequences. I believe we need to have a greater concern about the consequences of *not* being obedient to the Lord's instructions. Deliverance is central to the Gospel and not a 'specialised ministry'. We treat it with serious caution but also with wholehearted commitment, as we reach out to a troubled world.

Can a Christian Have a Demon?

This is an important question, and one that obviously causes a lot of controversy. I believe that the answer from Scripture, and from experience, must be an emphatic YES! Probably the more relevant question to ask is, 'Has that Christian made Jesus Lord of every area of their life and are they living full of the Holy Spirit?'

We see several examples from Scripture that help to shed some light on this contentious issue. Firstly, in the lives of Anani'as and Sapphi'ra. When their act of trying to deceive the apostles had been exposed, Peter says to Anani'as, *'Why has Satan filled your heart to lie to the Holy Spirit...'* (Acts 5:3). Here was a born-again Christian but an evil spirit had come into him which caused him to act in a deceitful way. Then again we see in Peter's life when he was trying to stop Jesus talking about going to the cross, the Lord turned to him and said, *'get behind me Satan! You are a hindrance to me; for you are not on the side of God but of men'* (Matthew 16:23). Jesus wasn't speaking actually to Peter, He was addressing the evil spirit that was speaking out of him. Also, as Paul wrote to the church at

Corinth, he warned them about the possibility of receiving another spirit, other than the Holy Spirit (2 Corinthians 11:4).

One other example is what was happening in the church at Galatia. Paul asks them the question, *'who has bewitched you?'* (Galatians 3:1). This is the standard Greek word which means, *'To smite with an evil eye'*. These people were saved and baptised in the Holy Spirit. They had seen God work miracles, but they were 'bewitched'. There was a sinister spiritual force at work in the church that had brought them back into bondage.

Often the argument is raised, 'How can an evil spirit dwell in the same body as the Holy Spirit?' It seems illogical. First of all we must accept that not all logic is truth, and some logic is based on a false premise. We could also ask, 'How can cancer be in the same body as the healing power of Christ's Spirit?' or 'How can a lustful thought be in the same life as God's Spirit of all purity?' The answer is that a person can have a demon without being demon possessed, in the same way that they can have a visitor in their home, maybe an unwelcome one. They could have a mouse in their house, or a flea in their clothing. They are not possessed by them even though they may be troubled or irritated by their presence, but they are there!

It is important to mention at this stage that we cannot blame everything on the devil and demonic powers. Sometimes it could be a case of emotional or psychological problems in the lives of those we are helping. With others, simply a lack of discipline and the need for self-control. To 'crucify the flesh' daily is a responsibility that can't be shrugged off by saying 'the devil made me do it'. Having said this though, I do believe demonic powers can ride in on these areas, particularly when they are not under the lordship of Christ. If people continue in wrong attitudes and thought patterns, or persist in habitual sin, then spiritual bondage can be brought into their life.

Doorways to Danger

Evil spirits need an open door to enter. They cannot just force their way into our life. We cannot catch one as we would a cold. Let us have a look therefore at some possible door-openers to evil spirits.

1. Involvement with Occult Powers

This could be in the past, or might well be a present involvement. Any dabbling with the occult in all its different forms is certainly dangerous. Perhaps through Freemasonry, playing with the Ouija Board, Tarot Cards, visiting fortune tellers, reading of horoscopes, yoga, hypnosis, séances, out of body experiences, levitation, acupuncture, mental telepathy, trusting in good luck charms etc. Even watching films or reading literature with an element of the supernatural in, can be the beginning of opening the door to bondage. The list is almost endless.

That involvement might have been in ignorance, simply for fun, or maybe out of curiosity. Perhaps in other cases it could have been a reaction of rebellion, or a search for help. Whatever the initial reason, bondage and oppression can still be the consequences.

I recall some years ago, visiting a Pentecostal church near Wigan. It was a midweek meeting and everyone in the Bible study were Christians. Right at the beginning of the service God gave me a 'word of knowledge' that someone was present who had been involved in the occult in the past and was under oppression because of that. No-one responded at the time but after the meeting had finished, an elderly lady came up to me and said, 'I was that person you spoke of.' She was a Christian, but said that she had felt bound for years. As a teenager she went along to a séance with her grandmother and since then there had been like a cloud of oppression over her life. As I prayed and took authority over the enemy she was slain in the Spirit, but when she got up again, she looked like a new woman, full of joy and freedom.

2. Unforgiveness

We open the door and give ground to evil spirits when there is an attitude of heart that continues in resentment and bitterness. In referring specifically to the anger of bitterness, the Bible says *'Give no opportunity to the devil'* (Ephesians 4:27). Sometimes a person can be like an emotional debt collector, keeping a mental note of what others have done or said. We become bound by the very thing we hold on to.

One lady who came into a meeting I was taking in Leicester was in exactly that situation. Throughout the service she stood out from all the other bright faces because she looked so oppressed. When she responded for prayer at the end of the service she shared that for ten years she had bitterly resented her own mother. As she renounced the spirit of bitterness and asked for God's forgiveness, release came from the bondage that she had been under for nearly ten years, and she went away a changed woman.

Another lady we prayed for at a Pentecostal church in Lancashire, came seeking help regarding her unconverted husband. She spoke of her resentment towards him and how they were constantly clashing. Before saying very much to her we started simply to pray in tongues and immediately without any warning the face of this Christian woman was transformed. Her eyes started to dart about, her face became contorted and she shrieked out with an ear-piercing scream! Her fingers were turned in like claws and she began to kick out and snarl angrily at us. As we took authority over the spirit of resentment and bitterness she renounced her unforgiveness towards her husband. It was then that deliverance came from the demonic power that was causing her to react so strongly.

3. Sowing and Reaping

We can open ourselves up to evil influences simply by the things we allow to be sown into our life. The Bible says,

*'Do not be deceived; God is not mocked, for whatever
a man sows, that he will also reap.'* (Galatians 6:7)

It could be through the television programmes we watch,
the books we read, the magazines we look at etc. Yielding
to temptation and remaining in a backslidden state leaves
us in a very vulnerable position. Where there are areas of
habitual sin and compromise, we can become open to evil
spirits.

I had a phone call one morning to go and pray for a
young man who was having a lot of problems in his life. As
soon as I arrived at the house, there seemed to be a dark
oppressive presence. We began to talk and the situation
seemed to be getting nowhere. I then asked if he had any
involvement with the occult and his reply at first was 'no'.
Later he admitted to a variety of videos, books and magazines in the house, which were about the supernatural.
After counselling he came to a place of seeing the danger
of these things and the effect they were having on his life.
He repented of this and was released as we burned them
together in the fire.

4. Inheritance

There is the possibility of the sins and influence of those in
our generational line affecting us, if those people have
been involved in the occult themselves. We read in
Exodus 20:5 *'For I the Lord your God am a jealous God,
visiting the iniquity of the fathers upon the children to the
third and fourth generation.'*

This was the case with a lady who came out for prayer in
Grimsby. She had been a Christian for nine years and
attended a strong Bible teaching Pentecostal church. Since
she'd been converted though, she just couldn't relate to
Jesus. Her prayers, thoughts and feelings were always
directed to God. There was no doubt about her salvation.
She recognised the importance of Christ and dearly
wanted to be able to relate to Him but just could not.

As we talked, it turned out that not only had she been involved with the occult in the past, her uncle and aunt were also strong spiritualists. I explained how this was the root of her blockage. She repented of the past, and as I took authority over the enemy and cut her off from the influence of her uncle and aunt she was instantly released. She said she felt it was as though something had left her. About three months later, I had a letter from her telling me how from that night on, her life was changed and she could now worship and love Jesus!

5. Emotional Trauma

Demonic powers take advantage when we are most vulnerable. So many people today have present-day problems because of past events, particularly when there has been a deep shock or intense grief in childhood; a bad car accident, abuse, or rape; perhaps the sudden death of someone very close, leaving a vacuum of fear and insecurity in the person's life. Also, continued rejection or domination by one or both parents brings damage to the emotions that evil powers can ride in on.

A middle aged woman at a meeting I was taking in Co. Durham looked very restless throughout the service. In coming for prayer, she shared that she'd been abused by her mother and raped by her father from when she was two years old until she was twelve. Later in her life she joined a witches' coven and made a 'pact' with Satan. Her life was completely devastated by all this and amongst other things she was bound by a spirit of bitterness and hatred towards her parents. When we started praying, demons immediately began to manifest, but by the end of the night she was completely delivered and even able to speak out forgiveness to her parents for the first time in her life!

6. Curses

The Bible says in Proverbs 18:21, *'The tongue has the power of life and death'* (NIV). Negative comments can be destructive in themselves, and do much to undermine a person's feelings of worth and self esteem. The old saying, 'Sticks and stones may break my bones, but names will never hurt me' is so untrue. Name tags and wounding statements can do great damage, especially when these words become pronouncements upon our life. If someone says something often enough we will begin to believe it. Statements like 'You're no good'; 'Your life will never amount to anything very much' can become a self-fulfilling prophecy.

There can also be a much more sinister side to this when evil people put a curse upon another person. It is then that something in the demonic realm begins to take hold of these words, and satanic power can be released to disrupt someone's life.

Many years ago a Christian lady went along out of curiosity, to see the so-called 'king of the gypsies'. While in a group attending this event she laughed at the gypsy. When he saw this he pointed to her and put a curse on her life saying that she would come to a 'sticky end'. Soon afterwards a throat condition developed and a growth started. Nothing seemed to make her better. Then one day her daughter reminded her of that contact with the gypsy and what he said. She came out for prayer at a meeting I was taking in Cheshire and repented of going along to this gypsy. As she renounced the words the gypsy had spoken, she said she felt herself giving a deep sigh as though a great burden had left her. It was then that her growth and throat condition disappeared and she testified to being completely free.

Steps to Release and Freedom

As we seek to bring deliverance into the lives of those who are troubled with evil spirits, it is essential wherever possible to do so with the help of at least one other person. There is both safety and greater authority over the powers of darkness when there is another believing Christian who can minister in faith with you. Also of course, you have the added benefit of another's wisdom and discernment in the situation. Having prayed together before the ministry session, claiming the protection and power of the blood of Jesus, the following steps are useful as a guideline.

1. The person being ministered to must wholeheartedly want to be free, more than anything else, whatever it takes. They need to be as desperate to be free as they are to breathe. If there is any sense of indifference, unwillingness or unbelief then this will be a hindrance to the deliverance.

2. We must help the person to be completely honest about areas of their past that might have opened the door to the enemy. The ground needs to be taken away from demonic powers by bringing into the light everything that might be relevant. If the person is hiding anything, they will only prolong their problem and delay their deliverance. This should never be hurried and much discernment will be required here.

3. When specific areas have been identified the person must then take responsibility for their sin by repenting, and renouncing it from their life. It is essential that any attitude of resentment and unforgiveness, even to those who have hurt them so badly, is confessed.

4. The importance of making Jesus Lord must never be overlooked. For them to find freedom it must be motivated out of a desire to live for Christ and not just to be rid of the effects of their problem. We need to look for the attitude of heart that expresses a complete, unconditional surrender to Christ.

5. We are now in a position to take authority in the Name of Jesus Christ over every evil influence in their life. By binding the influence of those demons that are identified and by breaking their power over the person, we can cast them out in Jesus' name.

6. The next step is to make sure that we ask the Holy

Spirit to fill their lives, so that the 'empty house' is filled with the presence of God. At this stage, encourage them to see the importance of continuing to live a spirit-filled life in obedience to God, no longer giving ground to the enemy.

7. A final step that mustn't be overlooked is for them to be willing to break with all forms of the occult. A good clear-out of their book shelves, record collection and anything that has association with the supernatural, needs to be destroyed. These things must be replaced with a commitment to feed on God's Word and to be disciplined in what they allow into their life.

11

Saved to Succeed

A story is told of a Texan millionaire who was holding a spectacular party. At the height of all the celebrations he invited anyone who had the courage to swim the length of his pool. The guests were all told that there was a prize for the person who could accomplish this. Either he would give a million dollars to the successful candidate, or the hand of his beautiful daughter in marriage. There was one draw-back he told them – the fact that a shark was also in the pool! No sooner had the offer been made than a splash was heard at the far end. As people turned to look, they saw a young man, striking out for all he was worth to swim to the other side. A crowd soon gathered and they all cheered him on excitedly, shouting, 'come on, faster, faster, you can do it!'

All this noise suddenly woke up the shark, who quickly realised that his dinner was rapidly disappearing up the far end of the pool. With a flick of his tail he surged through the water in pursuit of the man who was swimming with all his might. Just as the shark was about to grab him by the feet, he reached the side, where he was pulled out of the water in an instant.

A great cheer went up from the onlookers to acknowledge the man's success and courage. The millionaire then came up to him and said, 'Well done! That was marvellous. Now tell me, what you would like as your prize?

Do you want a million dollars?' To his surprise, the young man's response was 'no'. Smiling, the Texan said, 'so you want my daughter's hand in marriage?' Again the reply was 'no'. Puzzled by this, the millionaire asked, 'Well, what *do* you want then?' The young man replied, somewhat sharply, 'I want to know the name of the person who pushed me in!!'

'Accidental success' is never in God's divine plan for any Christian worker. His desire, for every disciple, is that they are successful in reaching their full potential, to reap His harvest. This becomes possible in our life, not through our own striving and self-effort, but it starts from the revelation that we have been saved not to survive, but to succeed! God wants to make something out of our life and ministry, for us to leave our mark in the history books of heaven. He is the God who delights to turn our failures into successes. He takes losers and makes them winners!

Weakness Can Be Our Greatest Strength!

We read in the Scriptures,

> *'Consider your call, brethren; not many of you were wise according to worldly standards, not many were powerful, not many were of noble birth; but God chose what is foolish in the world to shame the wise, God chose what is weak in the world to shame the strong, God chose what is low and despised in the world, even things that are not, to bring to nothing things that are . . .'*   (1 Corinthians 1:26–28)

This is certainly a reversal of the way that our world thinks today. In our 'macho', 'ultra-feminist' society, people feel they will get ahead and succeed because of their strong personality, independent attitude, sharp thinking and their outstanding abilities. More often than not though, what God accomplishes is through the weakness, frailty and insignificance of the ordinary things of life. That's why the Apostle Paul could say, '... *When I am weak, then I am strong*' (2 Corinthians 12:10). Sometimes we may feel that our words are very insignificant and our efforts very weak. Maybe we think that the things we do don't seem to cause much of an impact, or make any great change. However, what is sown in weakness can be raised in power, if only we'll believe in what God could accomplish through us.

This is well illustrated, when we remember what happened to Terry Waite, while he was held as a hostage by terrorists in the Middle East. Having been imprisoned in January 1987 until his release in November 1991 he was kept under appalling conditions. During this time, there must have been occasions when the darkness of despair swept across his life and he almost gave up all hope. Towards the end of that lengthy captivity, God spoke to a Christian lady in Bedford. He told her to send Terry Waite a postcard, with the picture of John Bunyan in prison and to write a short sentence of encouragement. She had no idea of his whereabouts and so put on a very obscure address before posting it off. The likelihood of this message ever getting through must have been a million to one. But somehow, when Terry Waite needed encouragement the most, that postcard made its way into his hands!

Eventually he was released and came back to this country. In that initial press conference he related this incident of the postcard. As he expressed how much it had meant to him, he said these words, 'Do not despise the little things that can be done'. Terry Waite knew only too well what that seemingly weak, foolish and insignificant postcard meant to him. As a result, he wanted people never to underestimate the difference a little effort on their part, could make in the lives of others.

Sometimes we can be tempted to feel, just like the lad who stepped forward offering his few loaves and fishes, to meet the need of five thousand hungry people. We may think we've not got much to give; there might seem to be little that we can do, but if we'll make available what we have got, as long as it's our all, miracles can happen! In the hands of Jesus, our resources can be multiplied many times over to meet the need of those around us and make an impact on the masses!

God wants us to be a success in every area of our evangelism. His plan of salvation goes far beyond having our blind eyes opened and being set free from the things that bind us. The Gospel not only rescues us from the power of Satan, it also releases us to fulfil the purpose of God! The Lord's intention for every Christian is that we might not just 'stand for Him', but be 'stirred into action', living with faith for a fruitful and effective life.

I'm sure we can all look back to some failure, or feeling of defeat and we know that the effect upon us can be quite dramatic. It is able to squash our enthusiasm so that we settle down for a mediocre life. Alternatively, it can cause us to strive in our own strength, to achieve, be accepted, or to be acknowledged as somebody. The experience of failure tends to make us feel inadequate, inferior, even insignificant to God. It condemns us and robs us of our confidence.

We can also be subtly influenced through things like the advertising world and especially the media of television. It is here that so many false concepts are presented as to what a successful person is. The images we see are often portrayed in very shallow, self-centred terms. For example, the beauty or strength of physical appearance, the importance of a person's intellect, talent and abilities, the material possessions that people have and the size of their bank balance. All these things as far as the world is concerned, are marks of 'success'.

Because of this distortion by our godless society, many Christians wrongly think that success is a 'dirty' word. Not something we should expect, or work towards, just simply be grateful if it happens to come along! One of the most subtle and effective lies of Satan is being sown into the hearts of Christians in this regard. Frequently, we hear it expressed in conversation as people say, 'God isn't interested in success, only in faithfulness!' This sounds spiritual and seems good, but all too often it's actually a 'cop-out' for how things are in a person's life, church or ministry. Success and faithfulness aren't mutually exclusive of one another, they go together. In fact I believe that one of the characteristics of real faithfulness is success!

God has said, '...*those who honour me I will honour...*' (1 Samuel 2:30). The way that God honours our obedience and faithfulness can be seen very clearly in the Scriptures. It is in terms that are practical, material, spiritual and evident to all. This is not simply for our own benefit, but as God works through the weakness of our lives, others will see His greatness.

Remember, God sent out Moses with just a stick in his hand, against the might and authority of Pharaoh, to bring release to those in Egypt. The Lord allowed David to go forward with just a sling and a few pebbles to slay Goliath; and God said to Gideon that defeat would be brought to the opposing army, not through a force of thirty-two thousand, but at the hands of three hundred! The purpose in each case was that God might receive all the glory through the success of their exploits.

The promise of God is that He will bless faithfulness in ways that can be seen by others.

> '*All these blessings shall come upon you and overtake you, if you obey the voice of the Lord your God. Blessed shall you be in the city, and blessed shall you be in the field. Blessed shall be the fruit of your body, and the fruit of your ground, and the fruit of your beasts, the increase of your cattle, and the young of your flock. Blessed shall be your basket and your kneading trough. Blessed shall you be when you come in, and blessed shall you be when you go out. The*

Lord will cause your enemies who rise against you to be defeated before you; they shall come out against you one way, and flee before you seven ways. The Lord will command the blessing upon you in your barns, and in all that you undertake;...'

(Deuteronomy 28:2–8)

Some might say this is just an Old Testament idea. However, we find the same principle in the New Testament, when Jesus said,

'By this my Father is glorified that you bear much fruit...'   (John 15:8)

The Lord wants us to be fruitful, in every sense of that word. In fact the more fruitful we are, the more He is glorified!

As we examine this further, let us consider three major aspects of success that will clarify what we are referring to.

What is Success?

This is an important question, because here is where a lot of misunderstanding comes in. A whole variety of wrong ideas have robbed, or at least restricted, God's people in discovering all they can accomplish for the Lord.

The best example of a successful person is the Lord Jesus Christ. His life was the fulfilment of God's plan and purpose, the Word made flesh for all to see. God said of Jesus,

'You are my Son, whom I love; with you I am well pleased.'   (Luke 3:22, NIV)

Now that's success enough for me! If the Lord can say the same of my life and work, then this will be the mark of my success and that's all I want, to be sure of God's approval.

The model of Jesus gives us the key to true success, in God's sight. In just one statement from Him we find the basis of all genuine success. He said,

> *'I glorified thee on earth, having accomplished the work which thou gavest me to do;'* (John 17:4)

From this verse we discover that:

(a) True Success in God's Sight is Always Judged by Motive

It is not so much what we are doing, but why we're doing it. That's the important thing. The first part of what Jesus said was, *'I have glorified Thee on the earth'*. The motive in the heart of Jesus in all that He did was totally pure and absolutely selfless. All His actions and words were to bring glory to God. We need to be able to answer the question, 'Why do we do the things that we do as Christians, particularly in our ministry and evangelism? Why do we want to preach the gospel, teach in the Sunday school, play in the music group and develop friendship with the unconverted. Why do we want to know God's anointing and bring healing and deliverance to others? The motive behind the choices we make daily and the plans we have for the future is important.

The reason why this is so vital is because of the challenge which comes to us in 1 Corinthians 3:10–13. Here we learn that when we are converted a foundation is laid in our life which is Jesus Christ. We then begin to build upon that foundation by the works that we do. With this in mind we read,

> *'If anyone builds on the foundation with gold, silver, precious stones, wood, hay, straw – each man's work will become manifest; for the day will disclose it,*

> *because it will be revealed with fire, and the fire will test what sort of work each one has done.'*
>
> (1 Corinthians 3:12 & 13)

There is coming a day when all that we have done and all that we are doing will be put to the test. The *'wood, hay and straw'* will be burnt up and only the *'gold, silver and precious stones'* will remain. What will be consumed by fire is the work that we have done with an unspiritual motive. Those things motivated out of the 'flesh', perhaps for our own glory, comfort or convenience. Only what is done with a spiritual motive, for the glory of God and good of others will remain. This I believe is the *'gold, silver and precious stones'.*

(b) True Success Must Be Seen in How it Relates to God's Purpose

Is what we are doing what God has given us to do? Jesus said, *'I have accomplished the work which thou gavest me to do'.* It's so easy for us to be busy doing all manner of good things, but the good has always been the enemy of the best. We can be taken up and involved in respectable, legitimate and commendable things, but miss God's perfect plan for our life. There must be an absolute conviction in our hearts that we are walking in the centre of God's will. Our time, energy and resources need to be channelled into what, 'God has given us to do'. Jesus, in reaching out in evangelism, was busy not simply with good works, but carefully following God's direction and fulfilling God's purpose.

Our work can look impressive, it can even be done in the name of Jesus Christ, but if it isn't what He has given us to do then it will mean nothing. When we don't live according to God's purpose and priorities, we can easily be deceived and misled. There just isn't enough time to fulfil our plans and also accomplish God's will! For this reason we need to make sure that God's purpose is central to our life.

The parable of the rich farmer gives us an example of someone who in the estimation of the world was 'successful'. He was hard working, conscientious and materially secure. So much so that he had to build larger barns to house all his crops. Although he looked successful in the eyes of man, this was not the case in the sight of God. He had left spiritual priorities out of his thinking and his life came to an abrupt end! Of this man God said,

> '...fool! this night your soul is required of you; and the things you have prepared, whose will they be?'
>
> (Luke 12:20)

The lesson we learn here is, what might look like success, could well be failure. On the other hand if we are obedient to God's purpose, what might appear to be failure, could well be success!

Who Can Succeed?

I believe the Bible gives us a clear indication of the sort of people who will be successful in their work and ministry for God. Their character has three important qualities.

Firstly, they *'delight in God's Word'*. The Bible to them is not merely a book, but something they love with a burning passion. It was said of Smith Wigglesworth, who certainly had a successful ministry, 'he loved the Word of God and he loved the God of the Word!' This attitude in our character is something that will always cause us to be blessed in what we do.

Success was guaranteed to Joshua when he took over the leadership from Moses. This promise though, was directly related to his commitment towards God's Word. God said,

> 'This book of the law shall not depart out of your mouth, but you shall meditate on it day and night, that

*you may be careful to do according to all that is written
in it; for then you shall make your way prosperous,
and then you shall have good success.'*   (Joshua 1:8)

Again we read in the Psalms, that our love for God's
Word will result in His blessing on all we do.

*'Blessed is the man who walks not in the counsel of the
wicked, nor stands in the way of sinners, nor sits in the
seat of scoffers; but his delight is in the law of the Lord,
and on His law he meditates day and night. He is like a
tree planted by streams of water, that yields its fruit in
its season, and its leaf does not wither. In all that he
does, he prospers.'*   (Psalm 1:1–3)

Secondly, they *'develop what has been entrusted to them'*.
We have all been given certain talents and abilities. The
problem is, not everyone takes the time and effort or even
has the confidence to develop them. In Matthew 25:14–30
Jesus told a parable about three servants who were given
by their master various amounts of money. It teaches that
they were expected to develop what was originally
entrusted to them during his absence.

When the master returned, he was looking for them to
have demonstrated their faithfulness, by increasing what
they were given. Two of the three had done just this, in
fact they had doubled what they were responsible for, and
the master was pleased. The third servant though, had
buried his talent in the ground and had neglected to use it,
and at this the master was angry. As we think of this the
scripture says,

*'. . . From everyone who has been given much, much
will be demanded; and from the one who has been
entrusted with much, much more will be asked.'*

(Luke 12:48, NIV)

Thirdly, they are, *'determined not to quit'*. When crushed by discouragement, and struck by disappointments, when frustrated by delays, they refuse to give up. They hold on to the promise of God's Word until it comes to pass. The prophecy they received, perhaps many years ago, and the vision that God had revealed to them, is something that they refuse to give up on. This is the heart of those who achieve things for God. In spite of the circumstances, they know that in Christ their destiny is never failure, poverty, defeat and shame. They live expecting God's Word to be fulfilled in their life.

The road to success may take some time and have many disappointments along the way, but don't give up at the setbacks and failures, because 'God is for you!' Always remember that champions are not those who never fail, but those who never quit!!

One of the greatest success stories in the Bible is found in the life of Joseph. He had received a tremendous revelation of his life being used by God. His success was going to be so great, that even his own father and brothers were going to bow down to him. From when this was revealed to him, to the time of its fulfilment, everything went wrong, but he knew God was with him. Having been rejected by his brothers and sold into slavery he was bought as a slave to serve in Potiphar's house. Even in this situation we read,

> *'The Lord was with Joseph, and he became a successful man.'* (Genesis 39:2)

While there, he was falsely accused of rape, after an attempted seduction by Potiphar's wife. This resulted in him being thrown into prison and just left for several years.

In spite of these circumstances, the Bible says,

> *'The keeper of the prison committed to Joseph's care
> all the prisoners who were in prison; and whatever was
> done there, he was the doer of it; the keeper of the
> prison paid no heed to anything that was in Joseph's
> care, because the Lord was with him; and whatever he
> did, the Lord made it prosper.'*   (Genesis 39:22–23)

Many a lesser person would have given up on that original
vision, but not Joseph. He remained faithful to what God
had shown him years earlier. As a result he was raised up
from the very pit of death, to the heights of being the ruler
over the whole of Egypt! His initial revelation was fulfilled
even to the extent of his father and brothers coming to
bow before him!!

How to be Successful

Having said all that we have so far, let me bring this
chapter and the whole subject of *Reaping God's Harvest* to
a close, in a practical way. I want to do this by looking at
some steps for people to take, in their desire to be a
success in whatever God might be calling them to.

1. Start Seeking God for His Specific Purpose for Your Life

For every believer God has got a plan and purpose. This is
not something vague and mystical but clear and definite.
Some people have 'good ideas' and their lives are full of
wishful thinking. If we are to be a success we need to have
a clear God-given purpose, something that we seek Him
for with all of our hearts. This will require that we change
our 'small mindedness' and begin to get 'hungry for God's
maximum'. As someone once said, 'Let us not be nibblers
of the possible, rather let us be grabbers of the impossible'! We will also need to change our confession if we are
to discover God's full purpose for our life. We must start
confessing, 'I am important to the Lord', 'He can use me
in a significant way'. 'God does want me to be successful!'

2. When God's Direction is Known We Need to Commit Ourselves to Working it Out

We shouldn't just expect God's plans for us to happen. We have to do something, God will not do it all! I believe one of the most important and necessary things for us to do, is to begin to take steps of faith. It's in taking these steps that we start to move beyond where we are at the moment. We begin to move forward in a specific direction and get to where God wants us to be.

Faith can often be spelt RISK and this is something that we must be ready for – to take a few risks. It is said that on the lunar surface is entombed a poster, with the words, 'Only those who risk going too far, can possibly find out how far they can go.' If we risk nothing, then we'll get nowhere. Let us have the heart of Peter, prepared to step out of the boat of our security, even at the risk of failure!

3. Never Make Success the Goal of Your Life

When we major on any one aspect of God's Word to the exclusion of other truths, there is always the danger of becoming unbalanced and falling into error. Whether we're talking about success, faith, prosperity, deliverance, healing etc. we need to take care that one thing doesn't become so all absorbing that we lose sight of everything else. To feed on a balanced diet of all aspects of truth is important here. As the Scriptures say,

> 'Man shall not live by bread alone, but by every word that proceeds from the mouth of God.'
>
> (Matthew 4:4)

Success for the Christian is never an end in itself. Our goal should always be to glorify God and finish well the work He has given us to do. This is where we need to look at our motives and repent of anything that doesn't put Jesus Christ first.

4. Ask the Lord to Set You Free From Anything That is Holding You Back

If a runner, be it in a hundred yards sprint, or a marathon, expects to be successful, he must remove anything unnecessary to the race. If he's dressed in a duffle coat and wellington boots there will be no chance of him winning! All the excess weight must be taken off. The same is so with ourselves. Anything that would weigh us down and be unhelpful in our life, has got to be discarded. God's Word says,

> 'Let us also lay aside every weight, and sin which clings so closely, and let us run with perseverance the race that is set before us...'   (Hebrews 12:1)

For some people it could be sinful habits or attitudes, for others it might be fear, unbelief, discouragement, confusion, or a sense of failure. We need to be honest before God and with ourself and not pretend that it's unimportant. Where there is something, we must acknowledge it rather than suppress it, or sweep it under the carpet. Only then can we press on to be a champion for God!

5. Have a Teachable Spirit That is Open to the Counsel of Others

The wisdom and guidance of mature men and women of God can be a tremendous help. They can see the situation in a far more objective way and be one of the means of God's direction, to keep us at the centre of God's will. In this day and age, where deception is so common and people 'feel led' into things that have never been initiated by the Lord, accountability to others is vital. The Bible says,

> 'Without counsel plans go wrong, but with many advisers they succeed.'   (Proverbs 15:22)

6. Commit Yourself to the Principle of Servanthood

True greatness comes from an attitude to serve other people. This is where the mother of the sons of Zeb'edee had got it wrong. Like any mother, she wanted her boys to be a success. The problem was she went about it the wrong way. Her request to Jesus was,

> '...command that these two sons of mine may sit, one at your right hand and one at your left, in your kingdom.'
> (Matthew 20:21)

Jesus replied by saying,

> '...whoever would be great among you must be your servant, and whoever would be first among you must be your slave.'
> (Matthew 20:26–27)

This attitude of being prepared to serve rather than be served and to be a blessing to others, rather than be blessed, will always, I believe lead to success.

The example of success coming from servanthood is seen in the life of Jesus, the greatest evangelist who ever lived. Paul writes of this principle by saying,

> 'Have this mind among yourselves, which is yours in Christ Jesus, who, though He was in the form of God, did not count equality with God a thing to be grasped, but emptied Himself, taking the form of a servant, being born in the likeness of men. And being found in human form He humbled himself and became obedient unto death, even death on a cross. Therefore God has highly exalted Him and bestowed on Him the name which is above every name...'
> (Philippians 2:5–9)

It is from this attitude of serving God and reaching out to those in need, that the Lord will bless our work and speak through us to others.

Someone who sought to follow Christ's example of servanthood and who was very much used to, 'reap God's Harvest', was David Livingstone. He had a brother called John, who had set his mind on making money and becoming wealthy. This he achieved, but under his name in an old edition of the Encyclopaedia Britannica, John Livingstone is listed simply as the brother of David Livingstone. And who was David Livingstone? While John had dedicated himself to making money, David had knelt down and prayed, surrendering himself to Christ. He had resolved, 'I will place no value on anything I possess, unless it is in relationship to the kingdom of God.' The inscription over his burial place, in Westminster Abbey reads, 'For thirty years his life was spent in an unwearied effort to evangelise others.' May God grant this also to be said of your life and mine in the harvest field for Christ!